Nesting After Divorce

CO-PARENTING IN THE FAMILY HOME

Beth Behrendt

UNION
SQUARE
& CO.

NEW YORK

**UNION
SQUARE
& CO.**

NEW YORK

UNION SQUARE & CO. and the distinctive Union Square & Co. logo
are registered trademarks of Sterling Publishing Co., Inc.

Union Square & Co., LLC, is a subsidiary of Sterling Publishing Co., Inc.

ISBN 978-1-4549-4979-4 (paperback)
ISBN 978-1-4549-4980-0 (e-book)

For information about custom editions, special sales,
and premium purchases, please contact
specialsales@unionsquareandco.com.

Printed in Canada

2 4 6 8 10 9 7 5 3 1

unionsquareandco.com

Interior design by Christine Heun

This book is dedicated to all parents who hope to break
the conventional expectations of divorce and co-parent in
a positive way for the good of their children and themselves.

And to all the nesting parents who've been paving the way
to a new approach: packing and unpacking, carting our
bags back and forth, and waking up so many mornings,
half-asleep wondering, *Where am I today?*
So our children don't have to. They can wake
every morning knowing that they are home.

Contents

Introduction

I will forever remember the moment the trajectory of my life changed. He was holding my hand across the table as we sat in the front window of our favorite local pub. It might have looked like a regular date night to a casual observer. But it was not. I was resisting the visceral urge to pull my hand free, and I could no longer look him in the eyes—the negative emotions were too strong. Instead, I averted my gaze to the reflection of the flickering candle in the window, and watched the heavy snowflakes pile up on the streetscape on the other side of the glass. Then he sighed and said the last thing I expected to hear, "Alright. I'm going to set you free. I'm going to let you go." I was flooded with relief that we were finally agreeing to end our marriage. Then I was immediately overwhelmed with fear and worry: What was this going to do to our three kids?

How did I—we—get to that moment? Well, a long time ago . . .

Bill and I met in graduate school at the University of North Carolina at Chapel Hill and started dating. We both got jobs in Washington, D.C., after graduation and married a few years later. People still tell us what a fun wedding it was.

Within a couple of years, we were enjoying our jobs, renovating a 1908 row house in the Capitol Hill neighborhood, and parenting a dog and thinking that made us ready to try the kid thing. I remember we were driving back from Home Depot, loaded down with the supplies for that day's house projects, when we made the decision to start a family. Bill noted how funny it is that the biggest and best decisions of life can sometimes happen in the most mundane ways.

Fast-forward fifteen years later. We had three young children. A lot of our life was good, but it was also stressful. We lived in an expensive city with young children and without any family nearby, plus Bill had long twice-daily commutes. We decided to move to my hometown of Fort Wayne, Indiana to save some money, be near my parents and my sister's family, and slow down. We found a sprawling 1949 mid-century modern home that we loved in a neighborhood close to a great school. It felt like the perfect place for our children to grow up.

Secretly, I hoped a simpler lifestyle and less financial stress would be the help our marriage needed. Things had not been great for a while. Sadly, our ingrained problematic behaviors seemed to have gotten worse with the arrival of children. My issues? Avoid conflict and full honesty; just hope difficult situations don't arise ever again. His? Deny depression and anger issues; just hope his natural charm would smooth things over after an outburst. Bill would erupt in anger, and I would unquestioningly placate or even lie to him. We made some short-lived attempts at therapy, but we just couldn't commit to overcoming our problems. It was easy to get distracted by everyday life and raising three kids.

In the almost eighteen years we'd been married, despite ongoing problems, I had never seriously considered divorce. "Divorce? I would never do that to my children!" I held the close-minded opinion that most divorced people were selfishly putting themselves above the needs of their kids.

But now I was beginning to worry that our marriage was hurting our kids more than it was helping them. I was growing convinced that the energy we were putting into saving our marriage was robbing the kids of the energy we should have devoted to parenting them.

I began to consider that divorce might be the only way. At the same time, I was racked with guilt that our divorce might cause irreversible emotional damage to our kids. The concerns were overwhelming: Would I be able to parent on my own? Would other kids at school make our children feel bad about having divorced parents? Would the experience set them up to fall into broken relationships themselves? Our sons were five, nine, and twelve. They fell smack into the age range (between three and thirteen) when divorce is considered to be most harmful to children.

"Children are resilient," people say all the time when it comes to divorce. But anyone who was a child of the old-school approach to divorce (heck, anyone who was a *child*, really) would probably strongly disagree. Current neuroscience and child development research indicate that children are not naturally resilient. Resilience is a trait that develops over time, and develops best in a stable, nurturing environment.

I had personal experience of being from a broken home when my parents separated for a time while I was in high school. Though they ultimately reconciled, recollections of the period of my parents' separation still haunted me. The worry, embarrassment, and sense of abandonment I'd felt all those years ago came rushing back to me as I considered my own divorce.

I didn't want to be the cause of those feelings in my beloved children. I hoped with all my heart to do things differently. But how?

I read countless books, articles, and blog posts about how to navigate postdivorce dynamics with your children and former partner. But so much of the information about co-parenting seemed outdated: "Dad gets one night a week and every other weekend." The advice seemed based on contentious relationships and making sure "you" got "your" way. None of it was giving me much hope.

One Sunday morning, I came across a review of a self-help book on divorce, called *It Doesn't Have to Be That Way*. That title alone gave me hope—*That's* exactly *what I keep wondering!* Once I had the book in hand, I devoured it. It was there I first encountered an unconventional approach to co-parenting. It was a lightning-bolt moment. *This is the answer!*

What was it? Nesting.

What is *nesting*? Keeping the kids in the family home after divorce, while the parents take turns caring for them; like how mommy and daddy birds fly in and out of the nest to care for the fragile baby birds, who stay put in comfort and safety.

Maybe you're already familiar with nesting because you saw that actress Busy Philipps and her ex, Marc Silverstein, Gwyneth Paltrow and Chris Martin, or Jeff and MacKenzie Bezos tried it as they divorced. However, don't be deterred: Nesting isn't an option just for celebrities and billionaires. In fact, ordinary people like you and me, all over the country—all over the world—are finding creative ways to make nesting work for their families.

Nesting has been on the fringes of divorced parenting for decades, but recent factors are leading to a groundswell of interest in this approach. First, changes in attitudes about divorce. Divorce is not going away, but the parents of today were often children who lived through a traditional, though traumatic, two-home approach to divorce and want to avoid that same fate for their children. Modern parents are more in tune with and aware of the importance of their own—and their children's—mental well-being. *Conscious uncoupling, positive divorce,* and *cooperative co-parenting* are common catchphrases and hashtags on social media these days.

Nesting co-parenting melds the contemporary surge in the positive divorce movement with a panacea for the anxieties of our current lives. These days, especially, families are fraught with anxiety. There is no denying that the coronavirus pandemic was detrimental to careers, financial situations, and the mental well-being of adults *and* children. Not surprisingly, the stress associated with the pandemic strained even the strongest of marital relationships. We're still learning how this fallout will affect marriages and families, but the indications so far are not positive. A report released in August 2021 suggests that divorce filings increased by 21 percent percent from the first year of the pandemic to the second; a larger percentage than ever before came from couples with children under the age of eighteen.

But nesting was a brand-new concept to me in 2013 when we were deciding to divorce. I excitedly shared this idea with Bill, who immediately reacted positively as well.

"It's not the boys' fault we're getting a divorce," he said. "Why should they have to suffer the stress and hassle?"

We hoped that by nesting we could keep the routine of daily life as consistent as possible for our children and give them continuity as we figured out what divorce would mean for our family. Of course, we knew that divorce would bring changes. We just didn't know yet what kinds of changes or how they would play out. We hoped that if the kids' day-to-day life didn't feel that much different, we could temper the fear and uncertainty of what was ahead.

Once nesting was on the table, the floodgates of creativity opened—as opposed to the traditional approach, which had made me feel that doors were slamming shut and options were being taken off the table left and right. Even though the divorce process itself was far from fun, figuring out how we could make nesting work for the boys was, and continues to be, a rewarding challenge. The idea of nesting also gave me hope that some of the many good things about our marriage could carry on for the good of our children.

For example, Bill and I both were and are close to each of our families. We enjoyed spending time with them, sharing traditions, and learning about the histories and memories of the older generations. We also had a strong commitment and attachment to our family homes. Each of our homes, first in D.C., then in Fort Wayne, had been given as much care and attention as we could offer—they were almost like members of the family. Lastly, Bill and I had always been good at tackling big projects together (Think *home renovations* and *three children*). We enjoyed creative and organizational challenges (Did I mention we met in graduate school for library science?). Nesting could allow us to continue giving our energies to these things we enjoyed—and were good at—all for the benefit of our children.

We began nesting in 2014. The logistics have evolved over time (see chapter 3, which outlines the many iterations of nesting my family has adopted, as factors in our lives changed and we needed to adapt), but we are still at it today. While our children were young when we told them we were divorcing, we were able to soften the blow by explaining to them they would keep staying in their home, just as always. As I write this, the oldest, Jack, is beginning his senior year of college, our middle son, Mick, is a senior in high school, and the youngest, Max, is starting eighth grade. Believe me, we have been through a lot of parenting stuff since we started down this path! I can honestly say that nesting is one of the best, if not *the* best, decision I ever made in my life—for my children, for myself personally, for both my ex and me as parents, and for our future as a family.

You may feel you're the only one going through divorce and trying to decide how to do things differently. I felt very much that way at that time in my life. Figuring it all out on your own is a daunting task. But you are not alone. Read on and you will find stories from other nesting families, as well as my own, to inspire you. There is also advice from experts—and lessons learned from other nesting families—to help you avoid common pitfalls and get through tough challenges.

This book will explore the many benefits of nesting. Among them:

+ Children don't have the stress and anxiety of going back and forth between two homes.
+ Parents don't have the stress and time expenditure of managing the children's lives between two homes (no driving to another house to get forgotten items!).
+ It's cheaper to maintain one family home as opposed to setting up and maintaining two homes large enough and sufficiently stocked for the children (who may only spend 50 percent of their time at either place anyway).
+ Less stress, more time, and more money allow each parent greater opportunities to pursue their own careers and interests.

Kudos to you for wanting to find a way to do things differently! Trust me: You don't have to figure out everything all at once. This book will guide you with a step-by-step approach to help you discover how nesting can work for your family. I want to help you find your way to a better and brighter future for yourself and your children!

CHAPTER 1

Two-Home
Conventional Divorce
and Its Traumatic Effects

The Recent History of Divorce in America

Little did anyone imagine, way back in 1969, how Governor Ronald Reagan's signing of California's Family Law Act—which made obtaining a divorce significantly easier than it had ever been before—would impact our society. Seismic societal changes grew from the way divorces would now be processed in California and these changes swept across the country as similar laws were quickly enacted in other states as well. Not only had the legal process of divorce changed, but it's impact on the lives of millions of people (particularly the children of these divorces) was, and continues to be, far-reaching.

This monumental change was truly a sign of the times. The 1960s were marked by a backlash against conservative values and traditional gender expectations. From counterculture hippies to college intellectuals to suburban housewives, everyone was questioning the status quo—and found many societal norms of the time to be either without merit or even downright harmful. Long-held beliefs about relationships and sexuality were shifting, and formerly well-established cultural expectations, like marriage and motherhood, were being reconsidered. Women were gaining more power over their education, life choices, and careers. It's no wonder that couples of that time desired to end marriages that they felt were keeping them from living their lives to the fullest.

California established a statewide task force to look at the relevance of existing laws governing family life. The task force determined that the state's divorce laws were too restrictive. Prior to the signing of the Family Law Act, a spouse had to prove to a judge that the marriage was worthy of dissolution, because of adultery, abandonment, or cruelty. The court had to be convinced that the end of the marriage was directly the fault of the other spouse. Essentially, a couple could only end their marriage if something had gone terribly and irreversibly wrong.

California's radical new law allowed for "no-fault" divorces: Spouses no longer had to prove that the other spouse had committed a specific act to warrant divorce. Governor Reagan accepted the task force's suggestion, the legislature passed the law, the governor signed it, and the legal part of the divorce process changed practically overnight in California. Across the country, people were overwhelmingly in favor of this change, and no-fault divorce laws were eventually recognized in all fifty states.

The result? Divorces immediately became *much* easier to get.

The assumption of the drafters of the original law was that easier access to divorce would set people free, allow them to undo early mistakes, and make better choices for their futures. Divorce was now considered just a minor upheaval in people's lives. Of course, many of the people seeking divorce were also parents. It was assumed that happier parents—who were now free to "find" themselves and explore the possibilities of a new life—would mean happier children. Surely the kids would be better off, it was felt, if they were no longer subject to the hostility, fighting, or quiet loneliness of their unhappily married parents. Because these children were the first generation to emerge from this wave of no-fault divorce broken homes, there was no historical basis for the assumption that happier parents meant happier children. This belief was based instead on guesswork and optimistic thinking.

The adults divorcing in the period from the 1970s to the 1990s had been children of the 1950s and 1960s, when the common refrains from their parents included "Pull yourself up by your own bootstraps," "Be a man," or "Act like a lady." Only after the publication of Dr. Benjamin Spock's groundbreaking *Common Sense Book of Baby and Child Care* gained popularity through the

1960s did parents begin to take a more nurturing approach to raising kids in ways that recognized what we now know about early emotional development.

But change was slow to come. Even through the 1960s, parents spent significantly less quality time with their children than they do today—and mothers were, by and large, the default primary caregivers. A 2016 study in the *Journal of Marriage and Family* reported that in the 1960s, fathers spent, on average, only *sixteen minutes* of quality time per day with their children. These cultural norms of gender bias were reflected in divorce court proceedings at the time. Judges then were guided by the precepts of "maternal preference" and the "tender years presumption," which declared that mothers were best suited to raise children. Therefore, custody of children in almost all divorce cases was awarded to the mother.

The giddy rush to divorce that began sweeping the country in the 1970s was basically an enormous, unplanned social experiment. Unfortunately, the understanding of the psychology of divorce did not keep pace with these radical legal and social changes. Instead, even after the national acceptance of no-fault divorce laws, people mostly hung on to the belief that divorce was expected—and even encouraged—to be nasty and vindictive. Divorce meant war. It was assumed that two people who had once loved each other now hated each other and would fight to prevail against each other at any cost—whether financial or emotional—and that the resulting emotional trauma to any children would have an only temporary effect, since kids were "resilient."

Before the passage of no-fault divorce laws, divorce was uncommon. Radical changes to the concept of how families could be configured were occurring with no history to draw on, or information for parents, and no way to help children adjust to their "new normal." Unfortunately, the idealistic optimism of the 1960s and '70s that was encapsulated in the mantras "Make love not war" and "Give peace a chance" had not proven itself useful in navigating complicated issues such as how to maintain a safe and stable home for children after a marriage ended.

From 1970 through the late 1990s, at least a million children a year witnessed the end of their parents' marriages. As time and research would show, children who grew up in the uncharted territory of broken homes were experiencing cataclysmic repercussions that would reverberate for the rest of their lives. Judith Wallerstein reports disturbing trends in her groundbreaking study that followed hundreds of children of divorce over a twenty-five-year span, from the time of their parents' divorces into their own adulthoods. In *The Unexpected Legacy of Divorce: The 25 Year Landmark Study*, written with Julia M Lewis and Sandra Blakeslee, Wallerstein shows that children from divorced homes had higher rates of learning problems and school dropout rates than their peers growing up in intact families, engaged earlier in sexual behavior and drug and alcohol use, and had higher incidences of anger and anxiety issues. Her study also reveals that grown children who endured their parents' divorce had lifelong difficulties forming adult romantic relationships: They marry less frequently, and those who do marry had higher divorce rates than the national average.

It has taken a generation and beyond to understand that the idea of no-fault divorce was done with the best of intentions—that is, to minimize suffering to family members. Yet the traditional model—where children are shuttled between two homes and left to fend for their own emotional needs while their feuding parents deal with their own crises—very often has actually done the exact opposite.

Traditional Divorce's Harmful Effects on Adults

In addition to the overwhelmingly negative (and now well understood) impact of such divorce on children, the emotional and psychological impact on adults who were divorcing is also now recognized. So, too, is the fact that the bad feelings surrounding a divorce do not end neatly when the money has been divided and the legal papers have been signed.

Divorce is not a finite event. This is a fact that is often overlooked by everyone, except the people who are actually going through the divorce. Even after the divorce has been finalized, there are lingering logistical, financial, and emotional issues to be dealt with, often for years to come. The ex-spouses need a readjustment period and time to focus on their emotional recovery. None of this comes easily, especially when parenting is part of the process. The postdivorce years can be far more difficult for the adults than originally anticipated, especially if the divorce was contentious.

There are crucial, interconnected pieces of postdivorce life to sort out: logistics (who lives where), finances (who pays for what and how), and parental concerns (who takes care of the kids and when). The decisions that were reached on all these issues may be clearly spelled out in the divorce settlement, but carrying them out in real life is an enormous task. They sometimes involve selling the family home, often buying or renting and moving to new homes, sorting out finances and new budgets, adjusting work and school schedules, and finding new jobs.

On top of all this, people who are newly divorced carry intense emotions and worries that can weigh them down for years. Society's propensity to judge fondness for judging divorced people and to focus on negativity only rubs salt in the wound of what is already an emotionally charged time. Even if the parent knew that divorcing was the right decision, feelings of guilt abound. It is difficult to ignore the frequently voiced opinions of others—both publicly and privately—that divorce is a selfish act that puts the parents' needs and desires above those of the children.

Society has continued to hold on to—and even promote—the punitive idea that if there's a divorce, there must also be someone who is to blame: In other words, there must be an innocent party and a guilty party. Therefore, guilt, shame, anger, and mistrust are now expected to be the primary emotions driving the actions of the divorcing couple. Exes are expected to attack and disparage each other—even if they don't truly hate each other—and the traditional approach to divorce does nothing to discourage this negativity and anger. Being filled with hate and resentment leaves very little time for hope, self-reflection, and moving on—not to mention good and involved parenting. Unfortunately, anger can remain the focus of the exes' interactions for years—and, for some, even the rest of their lives. Divorce is rarely the end of the feelings of animosity that grew during the marriage, and those feelings are exacerbated during a traditional broken-home divorce, when friends, family, and even society at large expect and encourage negative feelings and behavior.

Even when former spouses are angry at each other, loneliness and sadness over the end of the marriage are also common. Depression is normal in both men and women, since they must now face career, household, and parenting decisions without a partner. There may also be lingering feelings of love for the ex-spouse. But a conventional divorce fueled by animosity does not allow for the expression of—or even an acknowledgment of the existence of—any positive feelings, such as affection or a willingness to find common ground.

Oftentimes, in a two-home approach to divorce it is not uncommon—especially if neither person can afford to buy out the other's share of the home—for the family home to be sold to generate assets so each can buy their own residences. The loss of this family home can result in mourning for a place—especially if it was a home that was filled with happy memories before the divorce. For many people, home was a place of refuge and connection, a place where children grew up and traditions were made and celebrated. For many years before the divorce, the family home may have been considered the "forever home," with countless hours spent renovating, decorating, and landscaping it—in other words, putting loving care into it. The memories of that special place, and the knowledge that it is now being enjoyed by strangers, gives those who have gone through a contentious divorce another reason to grieve.

Another hurt in a traditional divorce living arrangement, which is also often unexpected, is the loss of connections with in-laws, extended family, and longtime friends. Losing this support network may leave the divorced spouses feeling isolated and questioning the strength of what they thought were long-term bonds with others. Friends or family members may feel that they need to take sides, and—being reluctant to do so—just stay away. Or family and friends may feel it's their place to express their disapproval over the divorce, adding to the guilt or shame each person in the ended marriage already feels. The traditional negative divorce, with its focus on division instead of continuation, encourages people outside the marriage to feel that they must take sides.

Last, but most certainly not least, parents worry about their children. Becoming a single parent after being in a two-parent home—whether the other spouse was particularly helpful or not—is a huge change. On the best days, parenting takes a lot of time and energy. To try to do so single-handedly—while also trying to build a new life, set up a second home, focus on one's career, and perhaps even start a new relationship—can strain the parent's ability to parent effectively. Children will be reeling from the changes in their world—especially if they have had to move out of their home and leave established friend groups or extended family—and may demand more attention from each parent than ever before. A traditional two-home divorce does nothing to encourage or facilitate a continued partnership in parenting once there is no longer a romantic partnership.

The complicated and challenging time following a divorce can stretch the parents' mental and emotional resources to the breaking point. Add to that the concern, perhaps even guilt, that the parents will feel about the changes to their children's lives. It is natural for them to ask: Did I make the right decision? Did we try hard enough? Did we prepare our children? How are they really doing? Do they need more from us? What will this divorce do to them? These are extremely valid concerns since, more often than not, these issues are not considered until *after* the divorce is finalized.

Traditional Divorce's Harmful Effects on Children

"Kids are resilient" is a common refrain divorcing parents hear. Are children really, though? Divorce is a very different experience for adults than it is for children. To the parent, divorce may feel like a huge relief—like a new beginning and the end to unhappiness, tension, and anger. To the child, divorce creates an environment filled with fear, anxiety, and uncertainty. Children need additional care and attention to understand the changes divorce brings to the family unit and to adapt to these changes in a healthy way, but the traditional model of divorce makes it very challenging to recognize and address these needs. Unfortunately, without insight into the value of addressing these needs, many parents simply expect the children to intuitively understand why their lives have changed and to adapt to the new situation in the same way that the parent is now adapting.

The role of parents—whether married or divorced—is to create as supportive and safe a place as possible for their children to grow up. After decades of research, the authors of *The Unexpected Legacy of Divorce: The 25 Year Landmark Study* observe, "In a well-functioning family mothers and fathers are in the background as their children grow up. From the child's perspective, children occupy center stage. A child's 'job' is to go to school, play, make friends, and simply grow up. The parents' job is to stay in the wings and make sure that the show goes on. They should of course encourage, applaud, feed, and clothe the 'players.' If the children stumble, parents should present a united front, come out of the wings, help them up, dust them off, and immediately go offstage again."

It's important for parents to remember that home, friends, and school are an anchor in children's lives and not to underestimate the upheaval that changing them will bring. Moving to a new home or a new neighborhood is not experienced by a child the way it is by an adult—it's much more traumatic. If the children have had to move out of the family home or can only stay in it some of the time, there is a loss of continuity and of a space that is consistently theirs, day in and day out. The children will also lose playtime and connections with their friends—either because they are not around their neighborhood as much, or because friends can't be bothered to keep track of where the child will be staying at any given time. Children may have had to move to a new home in a different part of town and have a new school and new friends to adjust to. In addition, the children now have the logistical challenges of keeping track of belongings between two homes. Holiday traditions will never be the same, and family celebrations may now be stressful and tense. The relationships they had with extended family—aunts, uncles, cousins, and even grandparents—may wither.

Experts say that the age of the children at the time of the divorce predicts many of the behaviors they will likely exhibit; the broken-home scenario only exacerbates these. Wallerstein, Lewis, and Blakeslee summarize the findings in their landmark study: "Age matters. Little ones, ages two to six, are terrified of abandonment. Elementary-school-age children, seven to eleven, grow resentful when deprived of opportunities they would have had if their parents had stayed together. Preadolescents, ages eleven and twelve, can be seduced by what Judy [Wallerstein] called 'the voices of the street.' Many teenagers, taking on the role of parent, become overburdened."

Children need consistent and steady support as they process the confusing range of emotions brought on by divorce: grief for their lost life; worry that they may somehow have been the cause of the divorce; fear that people can't truly be relied upon; anger that their parents made such a life-changing decision without properly explaining it to them; hope that their parents may reunite; confusion and anxiety over how their new life will come together; and sadness over having less time with one or both parents. They may also feel happy that they no longer have to see their parents fight or see them sad. It can all be overwhelming, confusing, and distract the child from the business of simply being a child. The chances of these negative outcomes occurring are greatly increased in a traditional two-households divorce, where the upheaval to the children's daily lives is both drastic and sudden.

The parenting relationship can change for the worse after a divorce, in which there are the complications of establishing a new life and home and struggles with residual animosity and bad feelings between the ex-spouses. In many cases, parents are so caught up in their own dramas—dating, freedom from the ex, maybe a new job or a career change—that their focus on parenting diminishes. The children become a backdrop to the parent's new life. Structure and discipline may disappear in a postdivorce life, where the adults are consumed by other seemingly urgent issues, and the children are left to basically care for and raise themselves. This creates further trouble down the road, when the parents may attempt to rein in or discipline their teenagers, only to find that they harbor great anger about the parents' previous absences or selfish choices—and they (quite naturally) question what right the parent has to now demand respect or expect to be able to exert control.

Wallerstein's study finds that another common change in the parent-child dynamic after a broken-home divorce is that a child may feel that he or she needs to move into a caregiver role with one or both parents. The parent, who now no longer has a co-parent in the home, may turn to the child to share confidences, ask for advice, or apportion out worries—all of which unnecessarily and inappropriately burden the child with concerns that are far beyond their years. Parents who rely heavily on a child for emotional or other support that is not appropriate for one their age (such as household chores or childcare for younger siblings) are rarely aware of the stress they have placed on them, or how alone and helpless this makes the children feel. Too often the children's daily lives have been overturned and no plans have been made to address their emotional needs. Those children may be unfairly burdened with the belief that it's their job to protect the parents, take away their pain, and make them happy—essentially, to serve as parent or even surrogate-spouse to the parent.

As Wallerstein's study shows, the experience of divorce can brand children forever with an enduring, heartbreaking legacy—one of anxiety, distrust, and low self-esteem. These issues can come back to haunt children in unexpected ways for years to come—affecting their emotional and intellectual development, their ability to form healthy romantic relationships, and even their future financial situations.

As I read the findings of Wallerstein's study, I found myself thinking about my own parents' separation in a new light.

I grew up in a conservative suburban town in the Midwest. Church—Protestant or Catholic—was the hub of most families' lives. You could find us—my parents and my younger sister and me—every Sunday in the front row at the 8 a.m. church service. I had little exposure to life outside our traditional community. Divorced families or single parents were seemingly nonexistent. The grown-ups kept gossip about divorced families and marital troubles under wraps.

Like most kids of my generation, my knowledge of the wider world came from watching sitcoms like *One Day at a Time* and *Who's the Boss?*, where I learned about divorced families. The kids all seemed pretty happy to me, but, true to the era, the dads were rarely around. That was hard for me to imagine because *my* dad was so involved in our family life: breakfast together before he'd drop my sister and me at school on his way to work in the city, family dinners every evening, and homework help whenever I needed it.

This perfect life came crashing down on the first day of summer after my junior year in high school. Dad invited my sister and me out to lunch—just the three of us! At the end of lunch, he told us that, though he loved my sis and me very much, he was going to be moving out. He just couldn't live in our home anymore. I cried in the bathroom after we left the table but pulled myself together to silently drive my sister and me home. We were both in shock.

The next afternoon as my sis and I were sunbathing "laid out" in the backyard (working on our SunIn highlights, no doubt), our mom came home from work, sat down next to us, and told us that Dad had moved out.

I was embarrassed for my mom, and for my sister and me—he had left *us*. Were we supposed to pretend that nothing was happening? I worried about whether my dad was still going to help me with my college applications. Would I still get to go to my dream college? Were we going to keep living in our house? Was Dad going to move far away? My sister and I were kept completely in the dark about what the situation was or what might happen.

And I was sad. I really missed having my dad around. We saw him a few times during that year, but mostly he was just . . . gone, like on the TV sitcoms.

Eventually, my parents did reconcile. After Dad moved back in, I was off to college and happy to distance myself from the whole thing. Sadly, it was a different experience for my younger sister. Though our parents had reunited, she was put through the same traumatic changes that most children of *actually* divorced parents went through at that time. The home we'd grown up in was sold and my parents bought a home in a different part of the city. My sister had to leave behind the friends she'd had her whole life and move to a much larger high school where she knew no one. Neighborhood, church, school, friends—everything we knew from our growing up lives so far was left completely behind.

My parents—kudos to them—had thirty-plus years together after that. I am so grateful that my children got to spend over a decade with my dad in their lives before he died quite suddenly from leukemia, just months after my parents celebrated their fiftieth wedding anniversary.

In all those thirty years, in true WASP fashion, my parents never spoke of that time again, neither to my sister or me, nor to each other.

I, too, buried the worries and shame away. Until one day—as I was now a grown-up and considering my own divorce—I found that I *needed* to remember those feelings from my younger days.

Those feelings would help me direct the course of my own children's experience with divorce.

Legacy of Childhood Divorce in Adulthood

The trajectory of a person's life can be drastically affected by their childhood experience of how their parents divorced. If it was a traditional contentious divorce, the now-adult children describe their parents' breakup as the formative event of their lives. After a traditional negative divorce, childhood is different, parent-child relationships are different, adolescence is different, and the transition to adulthood is different—in challenging and life-changing ways. The harmful impact of a contentious divorce on children—especially if their parents continue to behave badly toward each other in the post-divorce years—may actually increase and worsen over time as those children pass through new developmental stages later in their lives.

Moving into adulthood, children of difficult divorces may find that the adult decisions they now need to make—whether to marry or not, whether to have children or not, and how to continue a relationship with their own aging parents—are all colored by their memories of the parents' divorce. The lack of witnessing firsthand an example of two adults in a collaborative, respectful relationship restricts their ability to imagine themselves in such a cooperative partnership. They may feel disappointment in their parents' lack of role-modeling and struggle to figure out how exactly they will behave in their own adult lives.

Further, even as adults, children look to their parents for setting examples of good behavior and hope that they will continue to make their children's feelings a priority. In cases of ongoing anger between ex-spouses, the adult children of a contentious divorce are sorely disappointed. The parents' behavior at the time of the breakup of the home matters, but what matters even more is how the parents interact in the years following the divorce.

As adults, children of divorce may continue to be burdened by parents who have always put their own needs first, making it difficult for the normal process of separation between parents and children to occur. If the child assumed the caregiver role of a parent after a resentment-filled divorce, that role can be difficult to leave behind. The parent will have come to rely on the child as confidant and counselor and never made the effort to find a more suitable confidant. The grown-up child resents the drain on their own emotional resources but also feels guilty because they know the parent struggled after the breakup of the home and believe the parent has no one else to turn to.

Unfortunately, the roles that people adopt in childhood after a contentious divorce can continue into their romantic adult relationships. Caregiving children, once grown, may look for relationships that allow them to stay in that role—whether it's healthy or not. Children may find it harder to forge relationships and allow them to develop naturally over time. They either doubt their ability to choose the right person and pull away, or they are overly fearful of being alone and quickly jump into relationships that are unhealthy. They fear repeating their parents' mistakes and have trouble with conflict, because they never saw arguments resolved in the broken home—they only witnessed huge blowups or lingering, unresolved resentment.

When these adult children of acrimonious divorce are deciding whether or not to have children of their own, that decision may be fraught with worries. Their strongest desire is never to expose their own children to the kinds of loss and trauma that they themselves experienced as children of broken homes. They continue to envy friends and peers who grew up in intact families and fear that they may not be able to guarantee the same for their own children.

It's a common misconception to believe that a contentious divorce is a temporary trauma that is the hardest for the children at the time of the breakup of the family. Research shows that the effects are long-lived, and these effects change as children grow into adulthood. Children may be resilient, but the traditional approach to divorce destroys this natural resilience.

Putting the Past Behind

Considering all the difficulties outlined in this chapter, people almost never make the decision to divorce lightly. It's often the result of a long and intense conflict within themselves (and often with each other), as they struggle with the age-old question of whether they should stay together for the sake of the children.

Divorce can benefit adults while being detrimental to children, but keeping an unhappy marriage intact for the benefit of the children can be detrimental to the adults, who can spend most of their lives lonely and miserable. Our culture rarely addresses the full complexity of how to weigh these two potentially damaging outcomes against each other. It's simply easier for society to default to the outdated beliefs: Divorce means *one or the other spouse is at fault*; now *the exes hate each other*; *home life must be broken apart*; but that's okay, because *children are resilient*. These beliefs are still common, even though the evidence from recent history indicates that these views are gravely inaccurate.

Divorce is not going away. But we can learn from the mistakes of the past. The time has come to answer this key question: How can we make divorce better—for both parents *and* children?

There is another option besides the traditional divorce. An option that means less stress, less trauma, fewer hurt feelings, and less lasting damage to both parents and children. An option that helps to keep loving family relationships intact for years to come. It's an exciting co-parenting concept that is long overdue. Simply stated, the children remain in the family home and it's the parents who move in and out to take care of them. It's called *nesting*.

CHAPTER 2

A New and Better Way—Nesting

What a Happy Family Can Look Like After Divorce

During a transitional time, such as divorce, it is especially crucial for parents to provide a stable environment for their children with as few changes to the children's daily routines as possible. It is understandably challenging to focus on your kids' needs when you're overwhelmed with all the responsibilities of separating from your partner: the logistics, financial issues, legalities, and the emotional fallout. But none of these is as important as figuring out how to raise your children *after* the divorce—and how to continue providing them with the very best childhood possible.

A traditional, two-home divorce adds even more stress to an already stressful situation—for both you and your children. With nesting, children don't have to bear the additional burden of changing houses and keeping track of their stuff. Nesting can ease the transition for the kids to a new family dynamic. I believe nesting minimizes—if not completely eradicates—the trauma of divorce for the children. Marriages end, but this type of co-parenting allows the family to continue—and even thrive—after divorce.

Why Nesting?

A conversation on this very topic actually inspired me to write my first article about nesting. I was at the annual Fall "parents' night out" cocktail party for my sons' school—my first time alone at one of these since we'd divorced—when a couple who was new to the school introduced themselves. Making small talk, the wife eventually looked around the party and asked, "Which one is your husband?"

"We're divorced," I replied. "He's with the boys tonight."

Maybe this is a Midwestern thing, but it had been my experience that once I say the "Big D" word, other people look nervous and change the subject. But not Ashlie. She leaned in and interestedly asked, "Oh. What's your arrangement? How much of the time do the kids live with you?" (Guess she didn't get the memo on Midwestern reticence toward new people.)

By then we'd been nesting long enough (almost a year)—that I'd developed a quick spiel to describe it as succinctly as possible.

"What we do is kind of unusual," I said, and then went on to explain how nesting worked. Her eyes welled up with tears. I certainly didn't see that coming!

"Oh my God," she said, wiping her eyes and glancing with embarrassment from her husband to me. "If my parents had done something like that, it would have made such a difference. It's been thirty years, but I can still hear my little sister sobbing uncontrollably every time my dad came to pick us up. It was awful." Her eyes teared up again. "I'm so sorry I'm getting so emotional!"

"That's okay," I said, blinking back tears myself. "You just gave me hope that what we're doing might actually all be worth it."

How to Nest: A Brief Introduction

We'll delve deeply into all the logistical, financial, emotional, and other issues involved in nesting later in the book, but the two questions below are—by far—the most frequently asked by those who are skeptical that nesting could be a viable option.

HOW DO YOU AFFORD IT?

Nesting isn't only an option for celebrities or for the very wealthy. Families of all economic circumstances and from different parts of the country have made their personal versions of nesting work for them. They believe the shared-home model of nesting is cheaper than if they had taken the traditional, two-households approach, for two reasons: fewer possessions and only one primary residence.

Having the children remain in one home means there's no need for two sets of child-related things (for example, furniture, bedding, electronics, toys, bicycles, sports equipment, books, clothing, accessories, toiletries, medicines, etc.) in two different houses. This is a significant cost savings. All of the items related to caring for and entertaining children are only needed in one place: the family home.

As for real estate, the purchase and maintenance of two separate but sufficient homes (that is, homes large enough for raising children) is a huge cost. Renting a studio or one-bedroom apartment can be significantly less expensive than buying a second home. Depending on your area and housing needs, even two separate apartments may be cheaper than a second home. And, if the nesting situation includes one of the spouses staying with friends or family, or if it involves each of you continuing to live in the family home, the cost drops even more.

WHERE DO YOU LIVE WHEN YOU AREN'T IN THE NEST?

The options are wide-ranging and are limited only by circumstance, finances, creativity, and cooperation between the exes. Some common scenarios include:

- Each parent lives with family, friends, or with their new partner when not in the nest.
- Exes "share" an apartment during their non-nesting time (never actually being in the apartment at the same time).
- Each parent rents or buys their own apartment, condo, or small house to stay in when not in the nest.
- This is less common but, if space allows, both parents may continue living in the family home—in separate bedrooms and with other private space of their own, if possible.

It's important to keep in mind that the living situation that you agree on at the time of the divorce does not have to be the long-term solution—it can be a temporary situation while you figure out what will work best for each parent, the children, and all of you as a family.

The Benefits for Children
LESS HASSLE AND STRESS

In a traditional, two-home divorce, the children often live in a state of transience—never fully settled in either home. Or, one home is their primary residence and the other feels like a place they simply visit. They may prefer one home or bedroom over the other, but must constantly leave it behind. They never have *all* their possessions with them and must either learn to live without the item they forgot to bring or implore one parent to take them to the other home to retrieve whatever they left behind. They may be embarrassed at school by frustrated teachers as they lose track of homework between two homes. They miss out on fun with neighborhood friends as they regularly spend time in a different place. Their school may be farther from one home than the other, requiring waking up earlier and having a longer commute—or the distance may make it more difficult to get to and from after-school activities or sporting events. The experience of living at Dad's may be quite different than living at Mom's (or vice versa): Do they have their own room? Is their favorite cereal available every morning? Is there a gaming system to use when their homework is done? Do their parents subscribe to the same streaming services so they can watch their favorite shows? Is there a printer? Is the internet reliable? Can they have their beloved pet with them?

These may sound like minor inconveniences to adults. But children are not "mini-adults," and during the upheaval of divorce, the consistent daily life of nesting gives them a comforting sense of permanence. Though their family structure may be changing, their home life is not. Holly Rothenbush, a licensed marriage and family therapist and a board-certified behavior analyst in Fort Wayne, Indiana, summarized what she considers the benefits of nesting: "It gives kids the stability of 'This is my house.' It doesn't uproot them. Children need consistency. Yes, they can adapt to moving back and forth, but it is always a challenge." Something as simple as knowing that they will go to sleep in the same bed every night can be a great comfort. They have one place they call "home"—a home where they have the space, time, and freedom to focus on the person they are now and the person they are becoming.

NO DIFFERENCE FROM THEIR FRIENDS' LIVES

While we may discourage our children from comparing themselves to others, it is human nature to do so. This is especially true as children are moving into adolescence, when they are particularly vulnerable to feelings of inferiority and anxiety. As they try to figure out who they are and what sort of person they are becoming, they ceaselessly measure themselves against their peers. A 2018 study, published in the *Journal of School Health*, reports that of over four hundred early adolescents (grades 4–7), those with a positive self-image had the strongest overall emotional well-being—even more so than children who had lots of friends or did well in school (but didn't have a positive self-image). Children who have a positive concept of themselves are better at connecting with others—not only with other children, but also with adults such as teachers, coaches, and family members.

Young teens strongly dislike feeling "different" from everyone else. Children of two-home divorces may find themselves resentful of their friends with "intact" families, whose lives seem to be relatively easy and carefree. The child may be embarrassed at school by not having their sports equipment for the game and having to ask a parent to drop it off because the child forgot to bring it from the other home that morning. They've seen their teachers' frustration and felt their coaches' and teammates' annoyance. Friends may lose interest in trying to keep track of which home they will be at during any given time. Or they may feel embarrassed that their parents are divorced. They have heard grown-ups use the term *from a broken home*, and they know that it's not a good thing.

Nesting eliminates not only the hassles themselves, but also the feelings of frustration, embarrassment, and "differentness" that come with them. With nesting, the children's friends may not even know that their parents are divorced. As they compare themselves to their peers, they will see little or no difference. Very few "intact" families have both parents at home all the time, or at all sports or school events, or have both parents dropping the kids off or picking them up from playdates. Nesting allows the children to determine if and when—and with whom—they want to share the fact that their parents have divorced.

A CONNECTION TO HOME AND FAMILY HISTORY

The family home is the storehouse of memories. Home is both a symbol of continuity and a connection to a child's past. There, children are surrounded by all the possessions of their young lives and also by the memories of the surrounding location and the experiences they've had there: the sidewalk where they learned to ride a bike, the tree they fell out of (and the resulting broken arm), the playground where they played peewee soccer, the neighbor friend's kitchen that they know as well as their own, the corner store they are finally old enough to walk to on their own, the rock in the garden that marks where the ashes of their first dog are buried. Nesting keeps them firmly ensconced in the comfort of their own history.

The family home also offers a crucial connection to the family's history—and staying in it encourages children to see themselves within the context of that history. For a 2008 Emory University study about the benefits of sharing family history with children, researchers quizzed forty children, ages ten to fourteen, on family-history questions, such as where their parents grew up or what their grandparents did for work. Those children who answered more questions correctly showed less anxiety and fewer behavioral problems as the years passed. Nesting keeps the children surrounded by mementos of their past—and of their parents' families. And living with both parents (even if not at the same time) encourages continued references to these items and the telling of stories about their provenance.

The researchers who wrote *The Unexpected Legacy of Divorce: The 25 Year Landmark Study* comment that one of the saddest of their findings was that the children of two-home divorces did not feel a sense of continuity with the family history nor did they have memories—after their parents' divorce—of happy communal celebrations and family traditions.

Nesting means these positive associations don't have to change for the children. The family home can remain the center of traditions and celebrations. The specifics of how each parent participates may evolve after the divorce, but things like where the menorah is always displayed, where the birthday candles and wrapping paper are stored, or where the box of Christmas-cookie cutters can be found stay constant.

One of the things I love about nesting is that our three kids are constantly surrounded by reminders that we are a family. All our belongings, and the memories that go with them, accumulate in a home that's been lived in by a family for years. And I don't just mean the nice things, like the family photos we still have around. The random things that make us laugh over funny stories are even more important when it comes to imparting to our children key life lessons—even if they don't realize it at the time. I think those will stay with them the longest.

For example, we have this enormous and horribly ugly platter that belonged to Bill's parents. It's painted with a strange fish with fangs surrounded by some creepy squiggly eels with big eyes. They brought it out for the large Italian family Christmas feasts because it was the only thing that could hold the huge pile of spaghetti to serve everyone. That first Christmas I spent with them as the new girlfriend, I thought it was the weirdest-looking serving dish and got a lot of ribbing about how I just didn't appreciate porcelain "art." We all made fun of it—and me—every Christmas with them after that. In the sad days after they had both died and we were packing up the house, it was one of the things I asked if we could bring to our home (Bill and I were married by then and had a couple of toddlers). Now I can't imagine Christmas dinner without it. And, yes, the kids claim to be totally creeped out by it. Every year. And their dad points out that we all just don't appreciate "art." Every year.

More recently, my youngest was digging around in a desk drawer for something and unearthed a mixtape (yes, now you know I'm kinda old). Their dad made the tape for me when we first started dating. I thought I'd lost it years ago and was amused to see it again. That led to an entertaining (for me) conversation with all our boys that evening. I started with, "Observe, this relic of ancient technology—the cassette tape." Then I had to explain the intricacies of planning and recording a mixtape (in more detail than they really cared to hear) and the significance of it—especially if you'd just started dating someone and they took the time to make one for you! "No, it's not like making a Spotify playlist. And, yes, it has forty-five minutes of music: twenty-two and a half minutes per side." (God forbid you cut a song off by miscalculating and had to erase and start over.) They had some laughs at the music he chose. (Bill wasn't there to defend himself. But, in his defense, I can say the

Pogues' "The Sunny Side of the Street" is still one of my all-time favorite songs.)

Sure, these things bring us some laughs as a family. That's nice. But I think it's especially important, because we're divorced, for our children to hear about good memories their dad and I made together. Hopefully, these show them the reasons Bill and I ended up together, and why we chose to create these great kids together. These types of memories inspired us to create a divorce that is as positive as possible and honors the history that made us a family. Even though we're different from a lot of families because we're divorced, I hope the way we've designed this life for our kids makes them feel good about the strength of *our* unique family—quirky as it is.

Researchers from Emory University reported in their 2018 study, titled "Functions of Parental Intergenerational Narratives Told by Young People," that children were more emotionally healthy when their parents shared personal stories with them about coping with stress, anger, or sadness. An earlier study by the same researchers showed that children did better socially and academically if their parents described their own challenging times in "emotionally open" ways than children whose parents did not share such stories.

Nesting goes beyond just having a conversation about how parents have handled difficult situations—it *shows* the children, daily and in a context they fully understand. Though the children may not appreciate it at the time, seeing examples of their parents working together to make the best of a challenging situation—to benefit the children—is a priceless contribution to the children's emotional development.

Nesting also enriches the family by giving the children the chance to continue to build a robust relationship with each parent on their (the children's) own turf—not in "Mom's" house or "Dad's" house and not with the distraction of stepsiblings or stepparents. And the same is true of their relationships with their siblings. These relationships can develop and grow stronger through the typical interactions of arguing, competing, teasing, laughing, and rough-housing—in the safety, consistency, and comfort of the nest.

Stepparents and stepsiblings can be important relationships in children's lives, but experts agree that these are difficult relationships to build. They require hard work on the part of the parent and the stepparent, utmost respect for the children's feelings, and especially *time.* The American Academy of Child and Adolescent Psychiatry suggests that under the best of circumstances it can take up to two years for stepfamilies to fully adjust to life together. The challenges the academy outlines include: the parent and stepparent have not yet had time to adjust to their relationship as a married couple, the stepparents and stepchildren do not have a shared family history or a shared way of doing things, and the children may still be experiencing feelings of loss and confusion from their parents' divorce.

The American Academy of Pediatrics Committee on Psychosocial Aspects of Child and Family Health advises, "Within stepfamilies, it is unrealistic to hope that the children will immediately respect and love their new stepparents. In the real world, relationships develop more slowly. Children need time to really get to know and feel comfortable with a stepmother or stepfather." This is especially true with school-age and older children, "who are more set in their ways and may rightly feel that their established lifestyles are being disrupted by this new man or woman entering their life."

Nesting allows—even forces—a more gradual introduction of possible stepparents and stepsiblings to the children. They are not forced to move to a new home and face the possible challenges of sibling rivalry, competition for their own parent's attention, and loss of privacy.

As the *Landmark* researchers stated, "What most influences the child are the long-term circumstances of life in the postdivorce years." Nesting allows the kids' lives to develop with little to no distraction from the divorce.

The Benefits for Parents

Some of the benefits of nesting are immediate. Some emerge over time. All are far beyond what parents in a two-home divorce could ever hope for. Many nesting parents describe the immediate feeling of relief as they realize nesting is something that could work for their families.

LESS HASSLE AND STRESS

One of the most important benefits of nesting is that it's significantly less stressful for *you*. Yes, all the earlier parts of this chapter about putting the children first and focusing on making their lives happy, calm, and consistent through the divorce are valid and true. But you can't fully give your children those benefits if you are depleting your own energy, time, happiness, and finances.

First, let's consider the home. With only one primary residence—versus the two-houses scenario—there is only one property to maintain, manage, and spend money on. (The parents' non-nest homes are most often small apartments or condos that require significantly less care, are cheaper to maintain, and have lower rent/mortgages than a second, full-size home would.) Also, if either of you needs to travel frequently for work or otherwise, your home is never just sitting empty. If there's a maintenance emergency, like a leaking roof or a broken water heater, the other parent is there to address it immediately. If you have a pet, no kenneling is required. If you have a yard, a swimming pool, or appliances and devices that need maintenance, the other parent is there to tend to it (or to oversee the people you have hired to take care of it).

Second, let's consider all the physical stuff needed by children. You don't have to keep track of who has what, where it is, or how will it get from one house to the other (or to the school, the golf course, the music lesson, or wherever else it needs to be). Two-home-divorce parents spend significant energy, driving time, and money to keep track of (or duplicate) food, clothes, prescriptions, etc., as well as picking up and delivering forgotten items, which can result in being late to work or having to leave work in the middle of the day—not to mention the frequent driving between the two homes for deliveries and drop-offs. Nesting parents have only their own personal things to keep track of—the number and nature of which are undoubtedly much less than the countless things that one, two, or more children require to get through a typical week.

Third are the child-related communications. Everything—field trip forms, sports team picture forms, awards, flyers from school—ends up back at the nest for both parents to see. Or, if the communication is urgent, the parent in the nest is able to deal with it immediately. There is also the ease of simply leaving notes on the fridge for each other or the chance for quick chats as each of you moves in and out of the nest.

A SPACE OF YOUR OWN AND TIME TO YOURSELF

When you are a nesting parent who is "off-duty" from the nest, you can be truly free from parenting. The place where you go when you're not in the nest can be completely child-free, unlike in the second-home scenario, where there must be space—and stuff—for children to comfortably live there. At the non-nest space, there isn't any children's bedding or laundry left behind for you to wash—only your own laundry. There isn't someone else's clutter left around that needs to be straightened or put away—just your own clutter. A grocery run doesn't have to provide enough for the next round of children's breakfasts, lunches, and dinners—just whatever food (including adult beverages) you'd like to have on hand. Also, you don't need to get your non-nest place in order before the children come back in—because they won't. You can just walk out and lock the door behind you. Boyfriend left his razor in the bathroom? So what? It will be there the next time he visits. Dishwasher hasn't been emptied? No biggie—nobody's eating here tonight. Unfolded clothes all over your bed? You can deal with them when you return. Of course, if you have chosen to share the non-nest space with your ex, you need to be respectful and not leave the space a mess. The small time that requires, though, pales in comparison to the regular cleanup (and cost) of a full-size home stocked to house a couple of children or more.

As a completely child-free sanctuary, the non-nesting space demands very little of you. Of course, you are still thinking of your children—but this time and space can be extremely rejuvenating and lead to more patience and focus when you go back to hands-on parenting.

Freedom from child-related concerns can also be sanity-saving during a stressful and time-consuming process like divorce. Knowing that the children are well—living with routine and consistency in the security of the nest—can give comfort for you to focus, guilt free, on what you yourself need to heal as you move through divorce and into your new life.

FATHERS ARE NOT MARGINALIZED

In traditional divorces, fathers—even if they don't want to be—may be marginalized in the lives of their children. Despite advances in the fathers' rights movement and in equal co-parenting, fathers rarely get primary custody. Not being involved in the day-to-day lives of their children may create an emotional distance, whether that is the father's intention or not. This situation can occur for a variety of reasons; experts say the most common reasons are that the mother may want to "punish" the father for the divorce by limiting access to the children, or that the couple is simply defaulting to stereotypical roles.

Most often in traditional divorce, the mother remains in the family home with the children living with her the majority of the time. She continues the oversight of their daily lives and bears the bulk of their upbringing. Time spent with Dad may seem like a vacation to the children if he is less involved in their daily lives than their mother is. Dad's role may be to do the extraordinary with them—such as take them out to dinner and to fun events. Perhaps they do stay with him some of the time—but that home is not *their* home. This arrangement may not be at all what the father desires, but it is the frequent outcome of divorces.

Nesting simply doesn't allow this to happen. Dad has to continue to stay as engaged—if not even more engaged—in the kids' lives as he was before the divorce. When he is in the nest, he is fully responsible for their care—he *has* to step up. The laundry must get done, meals must be made, groceries must be bought, homework must be managed, and any scheduling that happens on his watch must be arranged. Kids are flexible, but they do best with consistency, such as regular bedtimes, healthy meals, a place and time to do their homework, and clean clothes that are ready for the next day.

Nesting involves fathers in ways that benefit children for the rest of their lives. The Fatherhood Project, a research program of the Department of Psychiatry at Massachusetts General Hospital, found in 2015 that children who had actively involved fathers had better adult outcomes. Adults who grew up with fathers invested in parenting were more likely to experience greater success in their careers and have fulfilling, lasting marriages. They also were better able to handle stress. For example, children with actively involved fathers were 43 percent more likely to earn A's in school and 33 percent less likely to repeat a grade than those whose dads were not as involved in raising them.

The Unexpected Legacy of Divorce: The 25 Year Landmark Study explains that the father-child relationship has an even greater impact in a divorced family than in a nondivorced one since "the relationship is unconsciously negotiated month by month, year after year, forged from countless interactions, until the son or daughter grows up. By the time they're adults, children of divorce have set opinions about how well their fathers did, whether they're worthy models to follow. Central to their judgment [are] feelings and questions that the children formulate over time. How faithful were you to me and my brothers and sister? Were you willing to give up anything to be my father? Did you make sacrifices? How hard did you try? What have you done with your personal life that I might want to emulate? Have you been civil with my mother? These are the children's yardsticks."

Nesting sends a very solid message to the children from their father after divorce: *You* are my priority. In fact, it may send even a stronger message than the traditional family structure in which— frankly—very few fathers are responsible for 50 percent of childcare.

Countless surveys through the years have shown the disparity between how much time each parent spends on childcare and household tasks. The Pew Research Center says that, in recent decades, even though fathers have increased the amount of time they devote to childcare, "American mothers spend about twice as much time with their children as fathers do."

A 2015 study, published in the *Journal of Marriage and Family*, showed that "mothers shouldered the majority of childcare and did not decrease their paid work hours. Furthermore, the gender gap was not present prebirth but emerged postbirth with women doing more than two hours of additional work per day compared to an additional forty minutes for men."

Even the pandemic lockdown, which forced many dual-career parents to work from home, didn't drastically change the situation. An April 2020 survey, conducted by Morning Consult, a business intelligence agency, found that while men and women were both doing more housework and childcare than before the Covid-19 pandemic lockdown, they weren't dividing the work any differently or more equally. In the survey, 70 percent of women said they're fully or mostly responsible for housework. Additionally, in couples with children under twelve years old, 70 percent of women were the parent "most responsible for childcare."

MOTHERS ARE NOT BURDENED WITH OUTDATED EXPECTATIONS

As a father becomes more involved with the children because of nesting, this means that a mother can be released from some of her responsibilities. The freedom from home care and childcare that nesting provides for mothers can be extremely liberating. According to the Pew Research Center, in 2011 fathers averaged seven hours per week on childcare; in contrast, mothers (including those who worked outside the home) averaged fourteen hours per week. Nesting makes these hours more balanced, which provides a significant uptick in the number of hours that a woman has to devote to her own interests—professional and otherwise. A new career can be more zealously pursued, or an existing one approached with more energy, or hobbies or other interests can be explored without the interruptions of children or the continual demands of home care of the two-households approach. Or, as many nesting families have found, one parent may offer to take on more childcare responsibilities to allow the other to focus on earning an income to benefit the new family structure.

IMPROVED RELATIONSHIP WITH YOUR EX

This may not be a benefit you are expecting or even hoping for as you consider nesting, but it's often a surprising consequence—even in relationships that appeared to be irreparably damaged at the time of divorce.

Every marital relationship is different, but many divorced couples report that their issues with each other had been preventing them from being the best parents they could be. Just because the parents remain together doesn't always indicate that the needs of the children are being given top billing. Nesting allows each adult to parent on their own—away from the distraction of their relationship with the other ex-spouse. This can lead to better parenting—and, even, a greater appreciation of the other's parenting skills. The relationship between exes changes as you move away from being a "couple" to being committed co-parents. Your history together can be a well from which you draw to nurture the continuation of the family, even though it no longer nourishes a romantic relationship. Successful nesting means that you need cooperation from the other person as much as they need it from you.

Successful nesting requires cooperation, communication, and (at the very least) civil interactions in front of the children. Yes, it does require that parents act like grown-ups and put aside their personal differences for the good of their children. (Further in the book, we'll explore how to make nesting work even when you and your ex do not get along.) Nesting forces you to get over your anger and hurt with each other much more quickly than moving into two separate houses might. There isn't really the opportunity to just drop the children in the driveway of one parent's house and drive away. The two-home scenario allows your relationship issues to continue unaddressed. Because of the cooperative nature of nesting, you are forced to learn how to better navigate these issues for the sake of the children (and your own mental well-being).

Nesting encourages you to accept the other person's presence in your life. Yes, it's a different kind of presence than when you were married, but it is still a constant that can't—and shouldn't be—shut out. This constancy shows kids that even though their parents are divorced, each parent still matters to the other and deserves respect, still has a valued opinion, and is still a crucial part of the family.

It's a benefit if you find that you and your ex have now actually become friends.

OPPORTUNITY TO PARENT POSITIVELY

It's a gratifying feeling to realize what an important lesson you are teaching your children. They may not consciously understand and appreciate what you are doing, but this consistent message of cooperation will have a positive impact on their lives.

When nesting parents interact in front of their children, it sends a strong message to the children. They witness their parents coming together over issues that relate to their children's care and well-being and the overall functioning of the family. This is something you can be very proud of! Allow this pride to alleviate some of your guilt over the divorce.

Because of the nature of nesting, both parents must "buy in" to the idea of giving it a try and commit to making it work. It's motivating to see your commitment and hard work come to fruition. You have deliberately gone above and beyond society's expectations of how divorced parents should conduct themselves. Your relationship as a couple may have failed, but your successful parenting relationship can allow you to be a happier person, more focused on your own needs and ready for new experiences and new relationships. The effort you put into nesting allows you to feel less guilt as you pursue your new life.

Even extended family—such as grandparents, cousins, aunts, and uncles can benefit. Unlike in a traditional contentious, two-home divorce, extended family may be less inclined to take one side over the other, as they see how the two of you are working *together* for the good of your children. And with the children always living in the same place, it's easier for extended family to have less confusion over "Where are the kids? And when?" and, ideally, feel that they can continue to see the children as frequently as they did before the divorce.

Be proud that you are *choosing* what kind of divorce you are going to have. You are choosing to divorce and co-parent with integrity, selflessness, and with focus on your children. You are choosing a model that is different than the outdated approach. You are choosing a model for raising your kids in the best way possible as well as one that benefits all of you—you, your ex-spouse, and your children—as your family evolves.

You are demonstrating the courage to make a good decision at a difficult time—to be a role model for your children. You are someone who has the courage to make a better life for yourself and for those you love. You are choosing nesting because you recognize that your children's health and well-being are your top priority.

QUESTIONS TO ASK BEFORE YOU CONSIDER NESTING:

+ Could we both agree to give nesting a try?
+ Could we come up with an option for living arrangements outside of the nest?
+ Do we consider each other good parents?
+ Are both of us generally mature, trustworthy individuals?
+ Could we work together to care for the nest—physically and financially?

If you answered mostly yes to these questions, then nesting may be a great option for your family!

Please also seriously consider:

+ Is one or the other of you—but not both of you—using nesting as a last-ditch effort to save your marriage?
+ Is there a history of untreated addiction or alcoholism?
+ Is there a history of refusal to treat diagnosed mental health conditions?
+ Is there a history of physical or emotional abuse?
+ Is there a history of pathological lying or illegal activities?
+ Do the children not want to be left alone with the other parent?

If you answered yes to any of these questions, nesting is *not* in the best interest of you or your children. Please seek professional advice as soon as possible to determine the next steps to protect your children and yourself.

CHAPTER 3

The Many Ways to Nest

There are as many different ways to nest as there are different types of families.

Beyond the desire to keep life consistent, financial concerns are often a factor that makes nesting appealing. Unlike the traditional two-home approach, which locks you into a situation that may be difficult to maintain from a financial standpoint, the variety of living options in nesting allows flexibility as you figure out what works best for your family. As you'll see in the examples in this book from other families, nesting does not necessarily require a large family home, nor does it require the purchase of a second (or third) residence.

We'll get into the nuts and bolts of how to figure out what will work best for your own family in chapter 4, "Agreeing to Nest with Your Spouse/Soon-to-Be-Ex—Step One." But to get the wheels turning, here are some examples of living arrangements I've encountered—or done myself!—in the years I've been writing about nesting and getting to know other nesting families.

Obviously, the children stay in the family home with the "on duty" parent. The "off duty" parent may:

+ Live with family or friends
+ Live with their new partner
+ Rent or buy their own place
+ "Share" a new place with the other parent (never being there at the same time)
+ Continue to live in the family home in a separate bedroom or another area of the home designated as their own, if space permits

In the family home, co-parents may each have separate bedrooms for their "on duty" time, if possible. However, some nesting co-parents switch in and out of a "shared" bedroom if an extra bedroom is not available in the home (changing the sheets and removing personal possessions from view on the change-over days).

In all of the above scenarios, consideration must be given to how to respect boundaries and allow for privacy for each parent, in the family home, especially, but also in a "shared" space outside of the home. We'll discuss how to make any of these arrangements work with as little stress as possible in chapter 9, "The Trial Period—Step Six."

As for parenting time schedules, again, they can be varied as the lives of the people setting up the schedule. Here are some examples:

- One day on, one day off
- Weekends only for one co-parent
- Weekends plus one night a week for one co-parent
- 2-2-3 (2 days in, 2 days out, 3 days in, 2 days out, 2 days in, 3 days out, etc.)
- 2-2-5 (same as above but with alternating 5 days out or in)
- One week on, one week off
- Two weeks on, two weeks off
- Three weeks on, three weeks off

As the above indicates, you can develop the schedule and living arrangement that makes the most sense for your family. Keep in mind, as well, that the schedule and the living situation may evolve: What is right for you now, may not make sense as you continue down the nesting path. You will learn from the other nesting families you will meet in this book, that their nesting situations evolved over time as their children grew older and as each of the parents' lives changed because of new jobs, new relationships, or other life situations. This has definitely been the case for us as, for a variety of reasons, the logistics of where Bill and I each lived has evolved over the years.

My Family's Nesting Life

Here's a snapshot of how our family's nesting life has evolved.

NESTING 1.0

When we separated and were discussing divorce and nesting, an obvious and easy start was for me to spend a few nights a week at my parents' house nearby. When it was my turn to be in the house with the kids, Bill stayed at an extended-stay hotel in town or drove over to Chicago to work from his company's headquarters and stay with a friend who lived there.

PROS:

+ The children's daily life stayed consistent: same house, same bedrooms, no change to their school or home life routine.
+ I had nice amounts of time with my parents, who were gracious and supportive as I was navigating the divorce.

CONS:

+ Bill found staying at a hotel depressing (and expensive). It could get complicated coordinating being at the office and staying with his friend, plus the wear and tear on the car.
+ I was forty-three and living with my parents; "gracious and supportive" only go so far—sometimes we fell back into the

dynamics of my teenage years (for example, one evening my dad "casually" commented about how many empty beer bottles he'd counted in the recycling bin).

NESTING 2.0

The above situation lasted about two months. But it was enough to see that keeping our kids in the house was working well for them and for each of us from a parenting perspective. I had been looking for apartments while at my parents' house and had found a one-bedroom place very close to the family home and the boys' school. Bill and I decided we would try sharing this space—never actually being in the apartment at the same time. We agreed it would be a good temporary solution as we finalized the financial aspects of our divorce and Bill looked for his own place. We sparsely furnished the apartment with extra furniture and household things from the family home. We continued to each keep all our personal stuff and clothes at the house—in the master bedroom—and toted a suitcase back and forth to the apartment. We established transition times as Wednesdays at 7 a.m. and Saturdays at 4 p.m.

PROS:

+ This was cheaper than renting two apartments.
+ For Bill, it was less logistically challenging than the hotel/office/friend scheduling

◆ I felt more like a real grown-up, as I was no longer living with my parents.

CONS:

◆ It was kind of a hassle to clean up the apartment before the other person moved in; and a hassle at the house to wash the sheets and clean up the master bedroom and bathroom before the other person moved back in.

◆ This setup may have made it more difficult to emotionally separate. Even though we were never in the apartment at the same time, and only briefly overlapped in the house, it was impossible to get away from reminders of the other person at either place.

NESTING 3.0

After almost a year, Bill rented his own furnished studio apartment in another part of town, still within a few minutes' drive of the house. I took over the apartment completely and moved all my personal possessions and clothing out of the house. The apartment became my home base and I switched to toting a suitcase back and forth to the house for my parenting time. The guest bedroom and bathroom became my personal space at the house. Bill took over the master bedroom and bath. We kept the same Wednesday-through-Saturday schedule.

PROS:

+ We each had our own personal spaces when we were out of the house, and when we were in it.

+ Dating became more appealing now that we each had our own spaces in which to entertain.

CONS:

+ It was more expensive to cover two apartments (even though they were both small and relatively cheap), plus the ongoing house costs—though we figured it was still significantly cheaper than if we'd had to buy and maintain a second house sufficiently sized and in the right location to move the kids in and out of.

NESTING 4.0

Another year of this arrangement passed, until Bill's job began to require more travel and he began dating a woman who lived out of state. It didn't make sense for him to rent an apartment that he now rarely used. Because his travel schedule was never consistent, we abandoned the set Wednesday-through-Saturday schedule. I would come to the house whenever he traveled—sometimes it was for only a couple of nights, sometimes it could be a week or more. We still aimed for 50/50 parenting time; but sometimes he would have to make up extra nights the following month.

PROS:

+ I continued to have my own separate space—my apartment—outside of the house.
+ It was cheaper than having two apartments.
+ Bill could travel a lot, knowing that the house was taken care of even when he wasn't in town. I dealt with any emergencies, scheduling contractors, routine maintenance, etc.

CONS:

+ Our parenting schedule wasn't as clear-cut anymore. Fortunately, the kids were older and just went with the flow. The oldest could drive himself. The younger ones just wanted to know who'd be picking them up from school or driving them around on the weekends.
+ My boyfriend (who himself was part-time parenting his son with his ex) and I no longer had a set schedule—it had been easy to plan dates and weekends away when we both knew we would be "kid-free." We had to adjust to an ever-changing schedule or make our plans well in advance so I could get it on the shared calendar with Bill.

NESTING 5.0 (AKA THE PANDEMIC LOCKDOWN)

And then the world shut down. March 2020.

The oldest, a freshman in college, came home to do remote classes. School went online for our middle son—a freshman in high school—and the youngest, a fifth grader, as well. Bill stopped traveling for work—though he was still putting in long hours from the office he set up in the house's master bedroom. Bill's girlfriend—she's a teacher so she wasn't going into school—moved in with us, too.

I needed to be at the house every day to help the youngest with online schooling. The schools were still working out the kinks of remote learning—it seemed that every day brought a new challenge or frustration that he couldn't have figured out on his own. Fortunately, the older two could handle the shift to remote learning—if our internet connection didn't crash, which was happening frequently. I also needed to feed everyone. (Remember those days of only one huge grocery-shopping trip every other week, then wiping down everything you bought?! Plus, no restaurants!)

Just generally trying to manage a house full of people (and an old dog who needed lots of care) required me to be there every day. Fortunately, I could still go to my apartment many evenings once Bill was done working for the day. But some days it was just easier for me to spend the night in my room at the house, so I could get up and make a good breakfast for the kids before 8 a.m. remote classes started.

PROS:

+ The fact we were already nesting made adjusting to how we cared for the kids pretty easy during this crazy time. People co-parenting in separate places had a much more challenging time (or just didn't get to see their kids while they waited out the lockdown).

+ Bill and I found it was no big deal to both be in the house together a lot, but it was important that we were clear on those days who was responsible for what with the kids, the house, and the dog.

+ I actually really enjoyed being with the kids every day. (The fifth-grade math, Spanish, and social studies "tutoring"? Not so much.) Life had really slowed down and it was great to be in our neighborhood and enjoy long dog walks together every day.

+ That said, if I hadn't had my apartment to escape to every once in a while—by myself, I probably would have lost my frickin' mind.

CONS:

+ We, none of us, had any idea how long this was going to last or how severely Covid might impact us and those we loved. It was a scary time. That sucked.

NESTING NOW

Lots of the pandemic era stuff has continued into how we nest now. I wanted to keep seeing the kids every day. So even on my nonparenting days, I pick the youngest up from school and spend time at the house with both of them. Or I'll spend a weekend at the house so I can help out with the boys, and Bill and I can work on house or yard projects. Bill still is not traveling for work. He'll visit his girlfriend or take short trips, but I frequently just "take over" parenting for a couple of nights and stay at the house even if he is there. (Though, don't get me wrong, I still do love my alone time at my apartment.)

WHAT NEXT?

Changes will come again. Either from something completely unexpected, or just from the kids getting older and leaving the house to pursue their own lives. Whatever the cause—because Bill and I have put a lot of thought and effort into keeping nesting rolling along this far—I'm pretty confident we'll figure out the next step that's best for all of us.

Meet the Nesters

The real-life nesters I met and interviewed for this book come from a variety of backgrounds, but all wished to share their stories to help others. As you learn more about their stories throughout the book, you'll see that nesting arrangements, like families, are not all the same. Their specific circumstances—the length of their partnerships, how many children they have, where they live—differ. However, what *is* the same is that each of these families is committed to putting their children first and were open to trying an unconventional way to do so.

LAUREN, BROOKLYN, NEW YORK

Lauren and her ex-partner's sons were eleven and fifteen when they began nesting. As with most nesters, Lauren says their reasoning for nesting was that "we both felt very strongly that the kids were not responsible for the fact that our relationship as a couple wasn't working. We were very committed to minimizing the impact on them, so nesting just made sense to us."

While they were nesting, the exes initially shared a furnished sublet a few minutes away from the nest (a co-op they owned together). Their parenting schedule was to switch out every other day; that is, one night in the nest, one night out of it. Lauren explained, "It may sound crazy, but it actually worked very well for us. Neither of us wanted to be away from the boys for more than a day at a time. If either of us needed to switch a day because of other commitments, we would work it out."

After a couple of years sharing the sublet, Lauren began living with her new partner in the Bronx when she wasn't in the nest;

her ex rented a room from a friend in an apartment nearby. They kept this arrangement for a couple of years, but now their oldest is away at college and the youngest will be leaving for college soon. They have sold their co-op and no longer nest. However, they were fortunate to find apartments one floor apart from each other in the same building.

KATE, TORONTO, ONTARIO

Kate's situation is rather unusual, even in the nesting community, in that she and her ex co-parented in the traditional two-home approach for several years *before* deciding to nest. "Nesting is sometimes promoted as a temporary solution right after divorce, but I think there is real value to the idea of nesting after the dust settles," explains Kate.

Initially, they equally shared custody and their two daughters, who were twelve and fourteen at the time, would go back and forth between their parents. Kate lived close to the girls' school and their friends; their father lived farther out and had a long drive in and out of the city to get them to and from school whenever the girls were with him.

"The kids preferred to be at my place, but I knew it wasn't because they were 'picking' me. It was just the easier place for them to be because of school and friends," recalls Kate. Her ex was trying to find a home closer to the school, but everything in the area was extremely expensive. Eventually it occurred to Kate to offer to rent him the spare room in her house.

They have been nesting for three years now. When her ex moved into the spare room, Kate began spending her time out of the nest at her partner's place, a ten-minute walk away. She frequently stops by the house to help out. Her ex lives with his girlfriend when not in the house. The parents switch in and out every week on Fridays.

"Even though we hardly overlap in the house, nesting renewed our sense of family again," says Kate.

MICHAEL, FALLS CHURCH, VIRGINIA

Michael, his ex, and their three children have been nesting in Falls Church, Virginia for over a year. Their children were eight, six, and three when they began nesting.

"It was spring of 2020 and I thought being in lockdown might actually help our marriage, but it didn't," explains Michael. "We began discussing ending our marriage and my wife brought up the idea of nesting. I'd never heard of it. I did some research and began to understand it better. I thought it would be workable for us from a logistical standpoint."

Michael still owns a condo from before their marriage. He goes there when he's not in the nest. His ex goes to her parents' house. Both places are within fifteen minutes of the family home. He and his ex switch in and out every other day. "But, because we have three kids, Saturday tends to be a 'divide and conquer' day for both of us. I might take one to a soccer game while she covers a birthday party. It's very important to us that our kids not have to miss out on anything because of the choice we made to divorce."

"The kids seem relatively unfazed by it all," says Michael. "As long as they're clear about whether it's a 'Mommy' night or a 'Daddy' night, they're fine."

SUZANNE, MAPLEWOOD, NEW JERSEY

Like Kate, Suzanne's situation is also rather unusual among nesters. She and her ex—and his new wife—all live in the family home with their two teenage children. They have built an addition to the home for Suzanne to have her own space—a separate entrance, bedroom, kitchen, and a sitting area with a door that can be opened to the rest of the house when she is on parenting duty (or closed when she is off duty or needs privacy).

Their children were four and six when the couple decided to end their marriage. Suzanne lived in the guest bedroom for about a year so she could be close to the children while she figured out other living arrangements. A frustrating day of house hunting sparked the idea of adding on to their current home instead of moving out. The couple agreed it was cheaper than getting another place, easier on the kids to stay in their home, kept Suzanne a part of the kids' daily lives, but gave her and her ex some separation from each other. While they were renovating, her ex's new girlfriend—now his wife—moved in with them. All three adults split daily parenting duties as needed and household tasks as they have deemed appropriate over the years. They alternate dinner nights with the kids and alternate weekends "on duty."

"I remember my son commenting when he was younger, 'Do you know that sometimes when people get divorced, they get *two* houses?!'" Suzanne says, laughing.

"Some people comment on what a lot of work this must have been—and still can be—and I realize, of course, it might not work for everyone," Suzanne notes. "But when I hear that I wonder, 'Wouldn't the kids feel burdened moving back and forth?' If you can find a way to accept the burden yourself, instead of your kids, why not do it?"

TEDD AND JEAN, NORTHWESTERN CONNECTICUT

Their children are grown now, but for over ten years the family nested on their farm in rural Connecticut. Their children were eleven and fourteen when Tedd and Jean—who had been together for almost twenty years—decided to end their marriage. Jean had the idea of finding a way to let the kids keep living in the family home.

"My immediate reaction," recalls Tedd, "was to say 'No, that sounds crazy.' But I thought it over for a few days and realized, 'This is kind of genius!' Why do we have to inconvenience our kids because we're not good married people?'"

When not in the nest, the off-duty parent stayed at Jean's mother's house. She lived just up the road and appreciated the company and help around the house. For many years, they parented on a two-week-on/ two-week-off schedule, but eventually relaxed the schedule depending on what was going on with the kids' activities or in each parent's life.

"We always did Sunday dinners together, though. And I think those were really important," explains Tedd. "Grandma would be over, and the kids' friends, and whatever boyfriends or girlfriends— of Jean or mine—happened to be hanging around. The parent leaving would make dinner; the parent coming in would clean up. It kept us all regularly connected and made new people feel welcome."

"I knew—once I got Tedd to 'yes'—we were capable of doing a good job with this arrangement," recalls Jean. "We always kept our eyes on the prize—whatever is best for the welfare of the kids. Tedd and I transitioned to a different relationship with each other, but the kids—our family—were always the most important thing."

Perhaps the above situations sound like fairy tales or something only the very amicably divorced could pull off, but they are all real people with real divorces and real parenting challenges. As you learn more about each of their stories—and my own—you'll learn more about the challenges and rewards of nesting. Our stories, along with advice from experts, will help you figure out if nesting is right for you and your family and how to make it work best for all of you.

QUESTIONS TO ASK YOURSELF AS YOU EXPLORE POTENTIAL LIVING ARRANGEMENTS:

- Could you share a living space with your ex away from the nest, e.g., a small apartment?
- Do either of you have friends or family with extra space with whom one or either of you could live when not on parenting duty?
- Do either of you know someone with a vacation property or AirBnB property that could be rented part-time?
- Are either of you romantically involved with someone else and could live with that individual when not in the nest?
- Would either of you be willing to rent space in a group home or a shared apartment when not in the nest?
- Do either of you have work that allows for travel that could be expanded to cover non-parenting time?
- Could you continue living together in your family home?

If any of these are plausible options—even temporarily—then it's time to discuss nesting with your ex (Step 1).

Questions to consider as you refine your living arrangement options:

What costs are associated with any of these options and what can you and your ex afford?

- ✦ Rent or purchase
- ✦ Furnishings and other daily living costs, for example groceries, utilities, parking, commuting
- ✦ Household contributions if living with family, friends, or a significant other
- ✦ Setting up or renovating part of the family home to define a space for the "off-duty" parent

Which of these living arrangements would allow for a parenting-time schedule that works for both of you and your children?

Who will be responsible for the different tasks associated with setting up the additional living space?

Most importantly: Can you and your ex pursue any of these options in an emotionally healthy and respectful way?

CHAPTER 4

Agreeing to Nest with Your Spouse/ Soon-to-Be-Ex—Step One

Sometimes nesting may not be a deliberate choice at first. Parents may stumble onto the idea in unexpected ways.

Jean, who nested with her ex and their two children for almost fourteen years, says that when they initially decided to separate, the plan was for her to live with her mom, who had a house nearby, and her husband would stay in the family home. The kids would move back and forth between the two places.

"When we explained this plan to our kids, my eight-year-old daughter's first question—this still makes me tear up!—was 'Will Pancake have to move back and forth, too?' Pancake was her pet hamster."

"That's when it hit me," says Jean. "If the hamster could stay in the house all the time, why couldn't we figure out a way to let the kids do the same?"

Michael explains that during the pandemic lockdown, "We were kind of nesting already because we were stuck together in the same house. We were taking turns being on- or off-duty every other night. The on-duty parent would be upstairs with the kids. The off-duty parent would spend the evening and sleep in the basement."

In most cases, the idea of nesting seems to occur to one parent first. It may be the same parent who brought up divorce or separation first, but not necessarily.

Since you have read this far, you're obviously doing your research. If you're the one proposing nesting, it might be a good idea to come prepared with some helpful articles—or this book!—at your initial conversation on the topic.

The First Discussion

The first conversation is critical, as your partner may have an idea already set in their mind of what separation and divorce will look like.

To help frame your discussion, these are the most important points to address first:

+ The benefits for your children
+ The financial benefits
+ Ideas on living arrangements and schedule

However, don't get too bogged down in details, which may overwhelm the other person or derail the conversation. Present the positives and give your co-parent some time to consider the option, do their own reading, and come up with their own questions. Nesting that's founded on a spirit of cooperation is more likely to be successful than if one parent feels it was forced on them.

In initial conversations about nesting, marriage and family therapist Holly Rothenbush suggests that a couple should try to answer some fundamental questions: Can we realistically be on the same page about parenting? And can we continue to work on our own issues and not take it personally if the other person says or does something with which we don't agree?

THE BENEFITS FOR YOUR CHILDREN

In your initial conversation with your soon-to-be-ex, you should first explain why nesting is the best option for your children, since it is less stressful than going between two homes and comforting for them to be in their own home and still feel like a family (refer to chapter 2 for more details).

"Nesting says, 'We value our family and our children's feelings above our own hurt feelings,'" says Rothenbush. "In so many divorces I see the parents get caught up in their power struggle and the kids come in last."

You know your children best and can tailor this part of the discussion to their specific needs. For example, our oldest son—who was twelve at the time we separated—had recently been diagnosed with ADHD. He was already struggling with keeping track of schoolwork and deadlines and the anxiety that comes with all of that. Bill and I were still working with him to figure out the right doctor and medicine to help him. Nesting was appealing to us because it was obvious that adding the stress to his life of moving between two houses would have been an unnecessary burden on him.

FINANCIAL BENEFITS

In this first conversation, you don't need to get into the details of how you'll divide every last thing and who will pay for what. It's better to focus on—as discussed in chapter 2—how nesting precludes the need to obtain a second residence that is large enough, as well as fully furnished and stocked, to support the children.

As Kate, nesting in Toronto, says, "Some people are critical of what they *assume* the economics of nesting to be. Nesting does not mean owning three homes. I don't see how anyone can think that doing things the traditional two-home way is more cost-effective. I'd encourage anyone considering it to really unpack the economics of their options."

Deborah Lansing, a Realtor with Keller Williams in Montclair, New Jersey, advises, "You may think you'll make a mint by selling the family home. But that might not be the case, and there are many things to consider."

Consider these important questions: What will it mean financially for one of you to buy out the other's share of the home? Or, if you decide instead to put the house on the market, what might the costs of commissions to agents, closing costs, and capital gains taxes take from the profit? There are also "hidden" costs before the home can go on the market, such as repairs and upgrades to the structure, landscaping, staging, and photography. You should also consider all the costs of renting, buying, and furnishing new residences for one or both of you.

And then there are the costs that are difficult to put a price tag on. The time and stress of preparing a house for sale; the emotions that arise from moving out of the family home and neighborhood; the time and stress of moving to and setting up a new home; and worries for the children if they have to move to a new neighborhood and/or school.

"You've got one life," says Lansing. "At the end of the day, what quality of life do you want for your family moving forward? If you really enjoy where you are and the kids enjoy it, then perhaps it's best to try to make it where you are."

LIVING ARRANGEMENTS

Again, you don't need to have all the answers in the first conversation, but if you have some initial thoughts about how the living arrangement could work—put them out there for discussion.

In chapter 3 we looked at some of the creative ways families have figured out to make nesting work for them—from having three separate residences (as Bill and I did for a time), to "sharing" another space (as Lauren and her ex in Brooklyn did at first), to continuing to each live in the family home (as Suzanne and her ex in New Jersey do).

Moving in with family—at least in the beginning—is often a choice that makes a lot of sense. After the "Pancake" incident Jean describes, they shifted their plan. She and her ex took turns moving back and forth to her mom's while the kids stayed in the family home all the time. "Grandma was all for it," recalls Tedd. "She had health issues and appreciated having someone around all the time to help her around the house."

Michael's scenario is a combination of a separate residence for him, and staying with her parents for his ex. "My ex initially suggested we continue to live in the same house. But I wasn't comfortable with that. I thought leaving for separate places would be better for each of us emotionally and would be less confusing to our children than if we both stayed in the house."

Ideas on where else to live may require some creative thinking on both your parts. Encourage your spouse to present their own thoughts on how the arrangement could work. It's fine if your first idea is just a temporary solution as you figure out your path forward.

When Bill and I first separated, I was staying at my parents', but we hadn't worked out where he would go when it was my turn to be in the house to parent. I suggested an extended-stay hotel in town, but that was pricey. Bill had the idea that he could visit friends who lived near his company's office in Chicago. Every other weekend he would hang out with his friends (less depressing for him than sitting alone in a hotel room) for a couple of nights and spend a few days working from the Chicago office (good for networking). He did this only three or four times until we began "sharing" our apartment, but it was an option that worked well as we figured out more specifics.

SCHEDULE

The initial conversation is also a good time to discuss what your parenting schedule might be—what factors you need to consider for yourselves, personally, and for your children. In our case, I wanted to see my children every day, but I was also trying to start my own business. I knew I would need some larger chunks of time to focus on that, so I suggested three and a half days out of the house for each of us. But because the boys were still pretty young and needed more homework assistance and regular dinner and bedtimes on school nights (when Bill was often in meetings until 7 p.m. or later), I offered to be in the house for more school evenings.

Whatever arrangement makes sense for you and your co-parent—and especially your children!—is the best one to start with. It can evolve over time, as needed. As you saw in chapter 3, this was certainly the case for my family, and for many others.

Before talking to your children, it's important develop at least an initial schedule to present to them. Réa Wright, a licensed clinical mental health counselor in Davidson, North Carolina, says routine and structure are essential to children's happiness. "Routine gives them a sense of predictability and emotional safety," she says. "You can build in flexibility, of course, but kids need the safety of a general routine."

Nester Michael recalls: "We had divorced friends not nesting—who were doing the 2-2-5 schedule, so we considered that. But my ex thought that might be a bit much for our three kids, considering their young ages. We do one night on, one night off, and tag-team when needed on Saturdays. When I'm off-duty I go to the condo I owned before we got married; she goes to her parents' house when she's off-duty. It was harder on me at first than the kids, because I missed seeing them every night. Unexpected things can throw off the schedule, of course, but now I'd say every other night is generally good for us."

To summarize, the goal for this initial conversation is to present the idea of nesting to your partner. Without getting too bogged down in figuring out the exact details, do address:

+ The benefits of nesting for your children.
+ The financial benefits of nesting for both of you.
+ Some initial ideas on living arrangements and schedule.
+ When to schedule a follow-up discussion.

Do not be too discouraged if the initial conversation isn't received as well as you'd hoped. Try to keep in mind that your partner may never have heard of nesting, or they may have an idea already set in their mind of what the next steps toward divorce *must* be. Ask them to just consider the idea for a few days, come back to you with questions, and be willing to engage in further discussion. As you may recall, our nester Tedd says that his first reaction when his wife brought it up was to say, "That's crazy!" But after thinking it over for a few days, he was fully on board. Michael, meanwhile, whose wife was already familiar with the concept of nesting, had never heard of it and needed a few days to research and read about it on his own before he felt comfortable pursuing it further.

Follow-Up Discussion(s)

After each of you has had time to process the idea of nesting, the following are the primary topics that will require further discussion. Again, these can—and will—evolve. You don't have to figure out every last detail yet or stick with something that ends up not making sense after all. You may find it helpful to draft an initial agreement in writing to refer to as you implement your nesting plan.

Susan Guthrie, an attorney and mediator in Chicago, says parents considering nesting should give serious thought to whether they have the patience and determination to follow through on the concept. "It takes very good communication, boundaries, and respect for a nesting plan to work and, therefore, parents must be committed to the process," she says.

TELLING THE KIDS

I imagine that telling the kids is foremost in your mind. However, as we delve into this more in chapter 5, "Talking to Your Children About Your Divorce and Nesting—Step Two," keep in mind that it is not advisable to tell your children about your separation or divorce until you have at least an initial plan in place to share with your kids.

Also, it's very important for you to schedule a time when you—*together*—can tell them about your separation and the plan to nest.

Jill Brakeman, a family attorney mediator in Litchfield, Connecticut, advises, "Have a plan in place before you tell the kids. If you don't have the answers, kids just worry. Sometimes you don't have everything figured out in terms of finances and housing until you have the mediation. But kids don't need to understand all that. They want to know how they personally will be affected, so have answers ready to their likely questions."

This initial conversation about the end of your marriage can be softened by being able to present—in that same conversation—how nesting will help keep their lives as normal as possible.

"The primary issue when children learn that their parents are divorcing is their sense of own safety," explains licensed counselor Wright. "They wonder: 'Who will be looking after me?' 'Who will tuck me into bed, take me to school, feed me?' 'Will I be okay?'"

This assumes that you and your soon-to-be-ex have both agreed to try nesting. If you're not in agreement, it's not fair to hint to your children that they may be staying in their home when that hasn't been settled.

When Bill and I sat down together to tell our boys that we were getting a divorce—they were twelve, nine, and five at the time—I immediately saw the fear in their eyes, especially the older two, who had a better idea of what divorce might mean for them. But they relaxed immediately as soon as I said, "But nothing's changing for you. You will keep living right here all the time." We were planning on a four-days-on, four-days-off schedule, so we presented it as a familiar scenario: It's like when Dad goes on a business trip for a few days and Mom takes care of you; or when Mom goes to see her friends and Dad's in charge.

It's very important for you and your spouse to be on the same page about what you will be saying to the children in the first conversation about the nesting arrangement. If you two have different ideas about specifics of your nesting arrangement (how long it will last, for example), either come to agreement before speaking to your children or agree to tell the kids that there are certain aspects you both are working on, and you will keep them in the loop as you figure things out.

HOUSEKEEPING RESPONSIBILITIES

This includes the nest, of course, but may also apply to another place that you are sharing with your ex, if you choose to go that route. We'll go into more detail about these in chapter 9, "The Trial Period—Step Six," on the logistics of sharing a living space with your ex. But, to start, begin thinking now about the two main questions:

+ Who will be responsible for which chores?
+ What would each of us expect the condition of the shared living space to be when we come into it?

Nester Suzanne outlines how they have divided chores at their shared home: "We split the cost of cleaning people who come in every other week, but each of us clean our own private spaces. He does most of the yard maintenance and I do the gardening. We trade off nights cooking dinner for the kids."

It may be helpful to examine your division of labor currently as you develop a plan for moving forward with nesting. In our case, Bill and I have stayed pretty close to how we divided chores when we were married. I handle most of the laundry and grocery shopping. Bill takes care of most of the regular house maintenance and repairs, and schedules service calls, contractors, etc. But we each have learned how to do *all* the chores and maintenance and can pick up the slack when needed.

We used to have a detailed list of what we expected on transition days. For example, at both the nest and our shared apartment: all dishes in the dishwasher, common areas vacuumed, sheets washed, bathrooms clean. We no longer share the apartment and at this point neither of us really cares so much about the state of the house, as long as nothing has been trashed and the kids have had their basic needs met. We've been at it long enough to understand that some weeks are crazier than others because of work or sickness or whatever. A completed cleaning checklist doesn't matter so much in the big scheme of things.

Now is a good time to think about *your* priorities, though, in terms of both of these questions. Maybe you will need essential grocery items replaced when you arrive so you can make the kids breakfast. Perhaps you want your ex to stash all their personal items in their own space so you're not looking at their stuff. Maybe you do *not* want to be the default laundry person or lawn mower. What are reasonable expectations? At least start the discussion.

COMMUNICATION

Whether you are nesting or not, co-parenting effectively requires a lot of communication. If you aren't already using a shared calendar, now's a good time to set one up and agree on what the color coding means. Some nesters have a physical calendar in the nest for the kids to see which parent will be on duty when.

You probably are already in tune with which methods of communication work, or don't, for your co-parent. For example, I know that if I send Bill a lengthy email—even if it has helpful bullet points!—he stops absorbing the information after about the second sentence. If I really need him to take care of something important or complicated, it's best for us to talk about it in person. Personally, I can't stand lengthy texts covering more than one topic. Just call me!

We both are big on handwritten lists with little check boxes for when things are done (did I mention that we used to be librarians?). I could probably wallpaper our home with the lists we've made for each other over the years. Since nesting began, we've always had the same spot on the kitchen counter where we leave a list for each other of upcoming kid stuff, like a pressing homework assignment or a friend's birthday party. When we began nesting, there were a lot of forms and announcements sent home from school on paper so those all went to the "list spot" on the kitchen counter as well. Now school-related communications are either emailed or on the school's website. I'm happy there are fewer trees being felled, but it is still time-consuming to monitor all the communications and send payments or fill out forms as needed. Make sure you discuss which of you will be reading and dealing with all school-related emails and forms.

A word of advice that I should have taken earlier myself: Don't try to change the other person's communication style now. Go with what you know works. As licensed counselor Wright comments, "The idea of nesting is a beautiful one. But the realities of it can quickly become difficult and complicated if the adults can't effectively communicate."

FINANCES

In these early discussions, focus first on home care and children's needs.

+ Who will pay for what?
+ How will we split agreed-upon shared costs (for example, groceries at the nest)?

Many nesters set up one account that they each contribute to, based on salary, for shared home and kid costs. When we first separated and divorced, we decided it was easiest—since I'd been handling the finances for years—for me just to continue paying for everything from our shared account. As we disentangled our lives, we disentangled our personal finances and settled on formulas (some of which were outlined in our divorce settlement, some that we decided on ourselves) for all the shared expenses. Bill keeps a spreadsheet of our house and kid-related spending, and we settle the difference monthly. Some nesters share access to a spreadsheet. In our case, I just email him a list of what I've spent at the end of the month.

FAMILY TIME

Discuss with your ex how you will help your children understand that you are all still a family. Nester Tedd mentioned earlier that family dinners on Sundays, their transition days, always happened and always included any other friends or family "who might have been hanging around."

Nester Michael says, "We still do each of the kids' birthday celebrations together. We both stayed at the house Christmas Eve. This year my ex was taking the kids on a trip for their spring break. She stayed overnight the night before their trip, and I drove them to the airport the next morning."

For the first year after we separated, Bill suggested we do "family movie nights" on Sunday evenings. It was technically his night with the children, but he suggested that some all-of-us-together family time was important for the kids. It was nice to all connect in a relaxed way that wasn't about a school event or extracurricular activities. Each kid took turns picking the movie of the week and we lounged in the den, watching it together and enjoying big bowls of my famous popcorn. (It just occurred to me that maybe Bill only *claimed* this was for "family time" and it was really just a ruse to get me over there to make him popcorn! Hmm . . .)

In all honesty, if we had recently had a contentious exchange, it was sometimes hard work—for us both—to be pleasant to each other. That was the good thing about it being a movie night: We could fake it (or Bill could stay in the laundry room "catching up on laundry" and avoid interacting with me at all beyond "hello") long enough for me to make the popcorn and start the movie. Then we could sit on opposite sides of the room and our lack of conversation wasn't too noticeable to the kids (hopefully) because the movie was on.

I know it may seem from this book that Bill and I always got along and had no problem spending lots of time together. We are there now, yes, but there were many times those first few years where we had to suck it up and be as pleasant as we could because we knew that was the right thing for the kids to see. We probably didn't do a great job of that sometimes, but we kept trying and eventually it got easier—Fake it 'til you make it, right?

If you aren't on great terms with each other, don't force more interaction than you can reasonably handle. But do try to have some, for the sake of your kids. Even something fairly simple, that doesn't require a lot of conversation between you and your ex, like taking the dog for a walk around the block on transition days or both meeting at the playground with the kids for half an hour once every couple of weeks, sends them the positive message that you *can* be around each other, and that you both enjoy being with them.

When you have your first conversation together with your children, you can establish that these are activities you will still continue to do together as a family, even though you will no longer all be living in the same home.

RULES AT THE NEST

We'll get into more of these in greater detail in chapter 6 on ground rules, and in chapter 10 on longer-term nesting challenges. While there are a number of "rules" to consider, these are *the* biggies that come up again and again for nesting families:

+ Can we, the parents, have overnight guests at the nest?
+ Or can we have a date over for the evening at the nest?

Everyone has different comfort levels when it comes to these concerns, but in my opinion it's best to just focus on being a parent when you're in the nest. I don't mean it has to be that way forever, and I certainly think it's fine to date all you want when you are out of the nest. In upcoming chapters we'll discuss how to handle dating as a nester, and how to introduce the idea of dating, and the new person, to your kids.

Also, if—and when—you begin dating, it may be best not to immediately introduce your new partner to your ex, especially if your new partner is one of the reasons for your divorce. No matter what happened between you and your ex-spouse before the new person entered the picture, I'm sure you can appreciate that seeing or being reminded of this other person will be a source of pain to your ex for some time. It benefits your children—and all of you—if your ex's energy is going into being a good parent, rather than being reminded of suffering and anger.

It's very common for nesting parents to agree on a timeline for introducing a new dating partner. Nester Michael explains, "We put in our separation agreement that we will not introduce the kids to anyone unless we've been with the person at least six months and we would let the other parent know before that happens. We also agreed that we would give the kids at least a year to adjust to the situation before overnight guests could be in the nest."

YOUR ISSUES AS A COUPLE

Challenges from your marriage don't just magically go away as soon as you separate. Unfortunately.

Even though Bill and I have been relatively successful at nesting for many years now, there are *still* times when our ingrained patterns rear their ugly heads. Not nearly as frequently as the early days, of course. Sometimes months or a year go by, but it still happens.

Not too long ago, there was an evening we were both in the house because he had a very late work meeting, so I came in to be on duty with the kids. He'd already done a few minor things to annoy me that evening, but what really was just too much—and if you've been married for a long time, I think you will understand how this could be the last straw—I was in the basement trying to get some work done and he was walking around upstairs *really loudly*.

In a split second my brain was on that old hamster wheel of, "God, that is so typical. It's *always* him, him, him. He has *never* respected me. This proves it once again."

And in that very rational mindset, I stormed upstairs to berate him for his horrible behavior.

His response? "Why do you *always* overreact? You *never* understand blah blah blah blah." (He may not actually have said "blah blah blah blah," but that's all I heard.)

I was near tears in my frustration.

Then Bill—I don't know how he did it because I wasn't able to—just pulled out of the moment and said, "You know what. When you and I have an argument, sometimes it's not just that we're arguing about one particular thing. It's like we're arguing about twenty-plus years of all the same things we argued about and didn't handle well before. It all piles up on that one thing and makes it a huge thing, right?"

Me, blinking away my tears, "That's for sure."

"And nesting probably makes this go on longer because we're just around each other more, right? It's like we're still married, but we're not—thank God."

Me, unclenching my fists and chuckling, "Right."

"And we wouldn't have done it any other way for the boys, right?"

Me, nodding. "Of course."

"We good?"

"Yep." I was.

So, yes, there are times that our long-running frustrations with each other come up again. This may happen somewhat more because we are nesting, but I imagine it is still a factor for most divorced people who must interact with each other because of their children. In the big scheme of things, I can deal with occasional frustrations with my ex, because nesting has been worth it for my kids—and for Bill and myself, too. However, I really would appreciate it if he would stop stomping around the house so much!

It's worth noting that therapy can very much help you avoid bringing the old problems of your marriage into your nesting life. This has certainly been my experience. Bill and I each continued to regularly see our own therapists for a couple of years after the divorce. I *still* see mine on an as-needed basis. Life throws other issues my way, but I do occasionally still need to talk over co-parenting and nesting challenges with her—even after all these years!

ESTABLISHING A TIMELINE

It's understandable to feel a bit overwhelmed trying to figure out everything all at once. Taking time to discuss with your partner your goals for nesting, the key steps, and a timeline for meeting specific milestones can help you organize the tasks associated with each step.

"After deciding if nesting will be helpful to the kids, the couple should set up a plan to 'test-drive' the plan and see if, in fact, it's a good fit for the children," advises attorney and mediator Guthrie.

You may tackle these milestones in a different order, depending on your circumstances. You may also have other items you believe are key goals. But—in my mind—these are the most important questions to answer as you move into nesting and toward ending your marriage:

- When will we tell the children about the end of the marriage?
- When will we begin our separation?
- When will we begin nesting?
- What is the length of time we will try nesting?
- When will we begin the formal divorce process?

In my case, I began at the bottom of that list. I had a specific goal and date in mind, based on the fact that our state required sixty days minimum from the date a divorce is filed until it can be finalized by the court. I wanted the divorce to happen as close to that sixty-day mark as possible. (Not everyone who nests is motivated to divorce right away. But I felt it was important for both of us, emotionally, to get the end of the marriage behind us so we could focus on the next stage of co-parenting and nesting.)

By the time we filed for divorce in mid-February, Bill and I had already agreed that we would separate and give nesting a shot. I was staying a few nights a week at my parents' and Bill was going to the Chicago office of his company a few days a week, to get the kids used to one or the other of us parenting them on our own. Here's what we had to do next:

- Find an apartment to share.
- Decide on a nesting schedule.

- ✦ Tell the kids that we were divorcing (but nesting).
- ✦ Begin nesting and set a date to review how it was going.
- ✦ Inform others—family, friends, kids' teachers—who we thought should be in the know, sooner rather than later.

We told our kids on February 15. I had already been looking for an apartment, so I had that lined up to move into that weekend. We began the nesting schedule the day after we told the boys. We informed close friends and family that weekend as well (more on how we did this in chapter 7, "Telling Family and Friends—Step Four"). We met with the kids' teachers the following week, to loop them on what was going on (more on that in chapter 8, "Assembling Your Team—Step Five"). The divorce was filed by my attorney on February 22.

Bill and I met at the one-month mark of nesting in March and tightened up some of our nesting guidelines and rules for the house. But most of my memory of that spring is just a blur of figuring out the management and logistics of the kids and the house and trying to start my freelance career. Plus, there were discussions, arguments, and so many texts and phone calls with Bill. And lots of therapy sessions (thank goodness) for me. For some reason I had decided to run a half-marathon that May (which sounds crazy, but I think the training was a great distraction from my worries and stress).

Our divorce was finalized on June 6. Not exactly on that sixty-day mark I'd aimed for, but seventy or so days isn't too bad, considering how many divorces I've heard of that drag on and on.

The length of the nesting trial period is up to you. Bill and I had that initial one-month review meeting. After that, we made some revisions and agreed to revisit it again in three months. At that point, we found we mostly liked how it was going and we agreed to meet every six months to work out any issues and think ahead to what was coming up in the next six months to a year.

When you decide to begin the divorce process is also your choice. We'll go into this in greater detail when we focus on the legal aspects of divorce and nesting in chapter 8. I was somewhat surprised to learn that many nesters wait years before beginning the divorce process. Both partners agree that the marital relationship is done and work out a separation and nesting agreement between themselves. They then go on to nest for their kids, date, and pursue their own lives for themselves until, for one reason or another—wanting to marry a new partner, for example—spurs them to officially divorce. Those who take that approach, like Suzanne, for example, explained that it just didn't feel necessary, nor was it financially prudent at that time to go through a divorce. For others, like me, it seemed necessary to make the divorce official for emotional reasons and for financial clarification.

Nester Michael and his ex moved fairly quickly toward divorce, as Bill and I had done. They took a similar approach to ours in easing the kids into being with just one parent part of the time.

"One of the things we did during the Covid lockdown," explains Michael, "was transition to 'Mommy nights' and 'Daddy nights.' One of us would spend the evening in the basement— read, watch TV, eat dinner, and sleep down there. The other one whose 'night' it was would do dinner and the nighttime routine with the kids. On weekends we started planning more things where all three kids would be with just one of us, and the other would have some alone time. So, by the time we had the 'Mommy and Daddy aren't going to be married anymore' conversation, we could say, 'But the only thing that will change, is that on 'Mommy nights' Mommy will be with you and Daddy will stay at the condo; then on 'Daddy nights' Daddy will be with you and Mommy will stay at Grandma and Grandpa's. In all honesty, they seem pretty unfazed by it."

All types of co-parenting can be challenging. Nesting relieves many of the burdens of the traditional approach to divorce and separation, but it has some unique challenges that you and your ex may face. Discussing these and developing a plan together will help prepare you both for successful nesting co-parenting. Therapist Rothenbush suggests three guiding principles for divorced parents: "Prioritize having a good working relationship with each other. Act respectfully toward the other parent. Keep the focus on the best interests of your children."

As nester Lauren reflects: "The main reason this has worked so well for us, although there was some anger initially about the separation, is that we have both always been fully committed to working together as parents. Our relationship ended because we weren't good together as romantic partners, but we never really fought. In some ways, nothing really changed with nesting. We get along well enough that we can overlap in the nest and spend time there together without any problem."

Nester Michael concurs, "No matter what the issues in our marriage, we were always really good at the logistical side of parenting and that's continued. We're both the type of people who put the needs of our kids first and foremost."

"What's interesting for me," he adds, "is that I find parenting a little bit easier. I was a present parent, but I feel even more present now with my kids. The marriage relationship energy no longer distracts from that. We both trust each other that we're making the kids the priority, but in certain instances we have different opinions. Now I have the freedom to chart my own course."

Prioritize together how best to help your children adjust to this new life, which will help you determine the milestones and timeline that work best for you and your family.

IN BRIEF: STEP ONE

It may take several discussions for you and your soon-to-be-ex to get on the same page about nesting.

Your initial conversation should cover:
+ How your children will benefit from nesting
+ Financial advantages
+ Potential living arrangements and parenting schedule
+ A timeline for coming to a decision about nesting
+ Plans for a follow-up discussion about how nesting could work for your family

In follow-up discussions with your ex, you should:
+ Begin to map out responsibilities: housekeeping, communication, finances, and rules of conduct
+ Be cognizant of ongoing issues as a couple and how to avoid them
+ Create a timeline for milestones as you move toward nesting
+ Decide if it makes sense to also pursue and file for divorce at the same time
+ Schedule a time to tell your children, together

It's critical to discuss with your ex any potential needs or challenges your children currently face or may face in the future, so you can both prepare in advance. Some concerns include sleep problems or nightmares, potty training, social challenges, difficulties at school, eating issues or disorders, and medical or emotional conditions that require medications.

Discuss how you as parents can prepare your children for nesting – and divorce, if relevant — in age-appropriate ways. You and your ex should:

+ Consider creating shared calendars (physical or electronic)
+ Establish what routines will help your children adjust, such as regularly scheduled nighttime calls or regularly occurring all-family events
+ Define the new logistics for your daily life, what will change, and what will stay the same once nesting begins

CHAPTER 5

Talking to Your Children About Your Divorce and Nesting—Step Two

You may be dreading telling your children about the end of your marriage. That's understandable. Perhaps it will be a comfort to you to know that most nesting parents find that it greatly softens the blow to be able to tell their kids they will be staying in their home and their daily lives will mostly stay the same.

Experts agree that it's important for *both* parents to be part of the initial conversation with the children. "If only one parent is there for the discussion, the children can't help but wonder what is going on with the other parent," says family therapist Holly Rothenbush. "You want to show them that we're still parenting together; the married part is ending but we're still a family together. I know it's scary for parents to be open with their kids—especially for hard conversations. But if there isn't open dialogue, kids just feel confused."

Beyond the importance of talking to your children together, this chapter will also go over:

+ Divorce from a child's perspective.
+ How to explain nesting to your children.
+ How to communicate appropriately with your children—
  what *to do* and what *not* to do.

Divorce from a Child's Perspective

As noted in chapter 4, "Agreeing to Nest with Your Spouse/Soon-to-Be-Ex—Step One," a child's first thought when they hear that their parents are divorcing is to wonder, "What does this mean *for me?*" You know your child better than anyone else in the world. Based on their personality, age, personal interests, and anxieties you can at least partially predict what their main concerns might be when they hear the word *divorce.*

With our boys, I thought about what they would like to hear to give them comfort about what nesting would mean to them. For the oldest, who, because of ADHD, already had a lot of anxiety about keeping track of schedules and all the things he needed to get through the day, a regular routine was going to be most reassuring to him. Our middle son is very self-sufficient but loves a lot of affection—he's a great hugger, but, even more than hugs from his mom and dad, spent almost all of his non-school hours snuggled up with the dog. The youngest was having trouble sleeping—he would end up in our bed almost every night.

"If parents can keep those types of worries foremost in mind as they talk with their children, it would make the conversation a lot simpler," says Réa Wright, a licensed clinical mental health counselor. "Every circumstance is different, but it's important to consider that a child's most basic foundation has been shaken. Children cannot articulate it in that way, but you as the parent know your child best and should keep that in mind as you talk with them. Reassure them that they will be safe and loved, no matter what happens next."

When Bill and I told our kids, the two oldest (twelve and nine) began immediately to cry at the word *divorce*, but calmed down as soon as we explained that they would be staying in our home, just as always. After the conversation, there were hugs all around. (Full disclosure: They hugged the dog before they hugged Bill or me—not taking it personally!) Then off they went to play Xbox together until family dinnertime.

There are no guarantees, of course, about how the news of divorce will affect your children. No matter how well you know your own children, they can still surprise you.

That we could immediately tell them in our "Mom and Dad are getting divorced" conversation that "Nothing is changing for you—you are staying right here in the house" was a huge comfort.

The oldest didn't need to worry about a changed schedule or keeping track of anything more than he already had on his plate—and it would all be in the same place every day. The only change to the routine was which parent would make him breakfast or dinner or drive him to school—the times and locations stayed the same. For the middle child, Mom or Dad were still available for lots of hugs—but, more importantly (I try not to take this personally), the dog is still there every day, ready for constant affection. The youngest would still have the same bedtime routine in his own room every night—and if he needed comfort at night we were still just right down the hall in the same place as usual. Bill and I actually took turns staying in the master bedroom when we were in the house for the first year after we divorced—primarily so the youngest could easily find whichever of us was in the house. After about a year, I moved to the guest bedroom on another floor. The youngest still had some sleep issues, but being a year older now, he was mostly okay with sticking it out in his own bed—if he really needed me during the night—making the trek down to my room.

Suzanne recalls, "It was about six months after my ex and I decided that our marriage was over and I began staying in our guest bedroom that we decided to tell our kids we weren't married anymore. It was a bit surprising because the five-year-old cried and cried. But we just kept reassuring her, 'Nobody is leaving!'"

In Tedd and Jean's case, Jean recalls, "Our kids were eight and ten. Our daughter's main reaction was 'Thank goodness I won't have to be away from the pets (the dogs and her hamster). I don't recall our son making much of a remark about it. Nothing was really changing for him."

"The initial reactions were interesting," says Michael. "The oldest wanted to understand what Mom and Dad 'not being together' meant, specifically. We explained, 'It means Mommy or Daddy gets alone time.' The six-year-old wondered, 'Who will snuggle me if I have a bad dream?' We explained that one of us will always be with you, and you can call the other one on the phone any time you want.' Which he did quite a bit the first few weeks. And our three-year-old daughter's reaction was, 'Well, I'll marry you, Daddy!'"

EXPLAINING DIVORCE AND NESTING TO CHILDREN

Even though our initial conversation about our divorce with the kids went smoothly, there was an unexpected hitch later on.

Bill and I had been nesting for about eight months. We had the same routine in the house with the kids every week. It seemed that we'd really hit our stride. Summer ended and the kids had their first days back at school (first, fourth, and eighth grades). It was my day in the house, and I picked them all up as usual. I was making dinner when the youngest said, "Where's Daddy?"

I barely glanced at him as I answered because it was, seemingly, such an innocuous question.

"It's my night tonight, honey. Dad'll be back in on Saturday."

Much to my surprise, he began to sob and cried, "I thought nesting was only for the summer!"

Oh my gosh, was I stunned! I hugged and comforted him, but, of course, I had to say, "No, honey, this is just the way it's going to be. Dad and I are divorced."

I felt awful. Had he been waiting all summer for Dad and me to go back to living in the house together? What had I said to give him that idea?

Our middle kid happened to be in the room when this happened. It had been my experience that the older brother is never particularly sympathetic to the younger. But Mick surprised me by kindly patting his little brother on the back and said, "It's okay Maxey. This is good. Everyone is happier now."

The youngest calmed down at that and dinnertime was the same as always. I didn't ask the youngest where he'd gotten idea that nesting was just a summer thing, but I did make more of a point the next couple of months of checking in on how he was doing and that he understood the situation. After that he understood what was going on and seemed fine with it.

But I have felt guilty about that moment for years. I still get a knot in my stomach when I remember it and have been kind of afraid to ask him about it. He's now fourteen, but what if he still remembered the trauma?

It occurred to me that if I was going to put this story in the book, I needed to talk to him about it. I screwed up my courage and asked him if he remembered that incident. I was *certain* he would, but as I described it, he just kept shaking his head, then laughed.

"I don't remember that at all! But I barely remember anything from when I was five."

"Well, you were six, actually," I said.

I got an eye roll, aka "Whatever," in reply.

I sighed with relief and thought—this proves how intense Mom guilt is—well, if absolutely nothing else comes out of this book, at least I know now that Max hasn't been scarred for life from thinking nesting was only a summer thing.

I learned two things from this recent experience.

+ If you're worried that you did something that hurt your child, don't be a chicken and wait eight years to ask them about it!

+ Even though I thought I had communicated about the divorce and nesting clearly to our kids, I shouldn't have assumed that the six-year-old understood it the same way his older brothers did. I should have taken a different approach to checking in with him.

As licensed counselor Wright explains, "Their reactions to being told their parents are divorcing depend on their age. How you explain things to them about divorce and nesting must be age-appropriate, too. Younger children, say, five to seven, don't know what it all means and may feel confused and scared. Older kids do understand and may ask questions, express anger and confusion, and be resistant and defensive."

There are some great books on how to talk to your children about divorce in age-appropriate ways (see "Further Reading and Resources"). While a children's book specific to nesting doesn't exist at this time, our therapists have some advice about how to explain divorce and nesting in ways suitable to children of different ages.

FOR THE VERY YOUNG

Therapist Rothenbush says, "For the youngest kids—five and under—they will just feel confusion about why there are changes. To explain nesting, you could use a picture book about birds and nests to show them how you both will be taking care of them while they stay safe in the nest."

"Really young kids have trouble communicating what they are feeling," she explains. "If you have concerns about how they are doing, a good therapist can help them communicate by using play therapy and drawing."

We can't assume that younger kids are taking in information the same way as older kids. So you may need to get creative in helping them understand nesting.

Michael recalls, "We told the kids there would be a schedule on the refrigerator so they could always know who would be there. But our middle child immediately began to cry, saying, 'But I can't read!' So, we now have stickers. I'm Chase and their mom is Skye from *Paw Patrol*. We give all of them a lot of advance warning about things like holidays that can throw the schedule off, so they aren't taken by surprise."

ELEMENTARY-SCHOOL AGE

Slightly older kids are better at articulating their feelings, but they may not fully grasp the situation. Rothenbush says, "For elementary school–age children, they tend to blame themselves for the breakup. They wonder 'What did I do wrong?' It's important to keep emphasizing 'It's not your fault.'"

When introducing the idea of nesting to children, counselor Wright suggests that it might be most helpful to gear the conversation to a child's feelings and emotions: "You could say, 'We're going to keep this as simple and easy for you as possible.' You can then explain to kids this age what the routine will be and show them a calendar of the schedule."

Wright also encourages consistency: "Still ask them to do their regular chores, and maintain the basics you would ask them to do under normal circumstances while also giving them some latitude for falling apart. Have them contribute to family life in age-appropriate ways."

OLDER KIDS: MIDDLE SCHOOL AND UP

"Older kids may feel a lot of resentment about the divorce," says Rothenbush. "At this age they can express how they feel, if you can get them to talk. I think most of them *want* to talk, but they don't know how to begin. Make clear that it's an open dialogue, as you discuss nesting, that you welcome their input."

Wright emphasizes, "Keep the lines of communication open. Tell them, 'We want you to talk with us. We know it may feel hard, but we won't be mad at you for asking questions or telling us how you feel.' Let them know that changes can be a struggle, but 'We'll do our best to make this work. Most importantly, we will love you always.'"

As for presenting nesting, Wright suggests, "Say to them, 'Here's what is going to stay the same for you and here's what will change.' You can then ask, 'What would you like to see happen as we are trying out nesting?' You need to come back to this conversation again and again so they know they can talk to you, and also feel heard and considered."

Stressing the importance of an open dialogue relates to the concept of "potted-plant parenting," which was hyped a few years ago. I've thought about this concept a lot as my kids entered their teenage years. We naturally spend less time together and they are less eager to talk with me. As a *New York Times* article describes it: "With teenagers, it's not always easy to know how to connect. By their nature, adolescents aren't always on board with our plans for making the most of family time and they aren't always in the mood to chat. Happily, the quality parenting of a teenager may sometimes take the form of blending into the background like a potted plant."

The premise of potted-plant parenting is that you don't force yourself and your questions on them. It's more effective to just find reasons to share the same space—without any ulterior motive on your part. Being near each other, and slightly distracted by other activities, can open the door to *possibly* interacting.

For example, my middle kid can drive himself now, so we are almost never alone just the two of us. He's recently gotten into baking, and we've started spending more time in the kitchen together. The first couple of times I was surprised that he didn't head back to his room for the thirty minutes the cake or whatever was in the oven. He liked to sit at the table and wait. So I stayed in there, too, and putzed around making a grocery list or whatever. Yes, he looks at his phone, but he also talks about what we're baking or about our dog. ("Why is he so weird looking? What *is* he?" is a favorite recurring topic of ours.) And sometimes he brings up something from school or a track meet or something another friend is doing . . . and we have a conversation!

(I'm a little worried that when he sees this part of the book he'll stop hanging out in the kitchen. But then it occurred to me—who am I kidding? He's never going to read his *mom's* book!)

Thinking of myself as a potted plant—one that somehow manages to put meals in front of them three times a day—amuses me. It also helps me keep my role in their lives in perspective!

COMMUNICATING WITH YOUR CHILDREN: WHAT TO DO, WHAT *NOT* TO DO

I know you may be feeling overwhelmed with all there is to figure out, but now more than ever this is an important time for you—and your soon-to-be-ex—to focus on your own mental health and general well-being as much as possible. The parents' state of mind and how they communicate with each other during this transitional time into divorce and nesting set the stage for how the children will handle their own emotions and develop their own healthy ways of communicating—right now and as they grow up.

"The emotional health of the parents makes or breaks how much the divorce will impact the child," says Rothenbush. "Sadly, some parents try to look better in the eyes of their child by bashing the other parent or blurting out things the child shouldn't be told."

Once again, I can't recommend enough a good therapist to help you through this time. Having a neutral party to vent to about my emotions regarding the divorce, was invaluable, but also having someone who understood the development and emotional stages of my kids was extremely helpful in guiding me on how to best talk with them. Countless times I turned either to my own or to my kids' therapist to ask advice on how to—or even if I should—broach certain topics with my kids. The therapists' guidance about how to start discussions in age-appropriate ways was always helpful, but what stands out in my mind even more are the times when they advised me *not* to discuss certain topics with them.

It's a fine line between being honest about your emotions (which is healthy for kids to see you do) and turning to your kids to be your emotional support. It can be easy to slip into venting to them, especially when you find yourself a single parent and no longer have an adult around with whom to discuss your worries.

"Don't put the burden on the kids for your emotions," says Wright. "The parents need to figure that out on their own."

For example, I learned with my therapist's help how better to express my worries to my kids. If I felt bad about being distracted and not giving them my full attention, it was okay to say to them,

"I'm worried about the roof leaking in the hallway, but Dad and I will figure out what to do." It was *not* okay for me to say (even though it's what I really was thinking), "I'm worried about the roof leaking in the hallway because Dad will be mad that I'm asking him to spend more money." I always took a beat before I said something to my kids related to the divorce or nesting, and I recommend doing the same.

- DON'T overshare. Children do not need to know everything you are dealing with.
  - DO share your adult problems with an appropriate adult, such as a trusted friend or your therapist.
- DON'T use your child as a source of emotional support or as your confidant.
  - DO express your feelings in a healthy way, and encourage your kids to do the same.
- DON'T put your child in the middle of disputes between your ex and you.
  - DO interact calmly with each other in front of the kids, say nice things about the other parent when they are not there, and encourage your kids to have a good relationship with the other parent.
  - DO spend time with your child doing things they like. That's especially important as you are transitioning into divorce and nesting.

As nester Michael says, "Our oldest especially values one-on-one time with me right now, so we get together to shoot hoops or I'll take him to basketball practice even if it's not my night. It's really important for us to have time—just the two of us—right now."

Finally, *don't* be too hard on yourself. A child's challenging emotions don't necessarily stem from the divorce. Just being a kid can be difficult and frustrating sometimes.

Michael describes a couple of incidents that remind him of this fact. "Over the summer our nine-year-old was having a complete meltdown, uncharacteristically bad. I had to wonder, and asked, if it had anything to do with 'what was going on with Mommy and Daddy.' He replied, 'No! It's that my brother is being a complete butthead!'"

Michael continues: "We are having our middle son see a family therapist because of some school issues and also so he could have a space to talk about the divorce if he wanted to. The therapist knows about the divorce, of course, and asked him: 'Have there been any changes in your life that have made you feel anxious or worried?' He answered, 'Yes! Because of Covid we have to sit in alphabetical order at lunchtime and I have to sit at a table of girls!'"

Your kids are probably not thinking about the divorce as much as you think they are, but you also never know when it might occur to your kid that they do want to know more.

One afternoon after school this past year, I was driving my youngest (yes, the one I thought had been deeply traumatized at the end of that first summer of our nesting) around after school. He was chatting away about the various things that go through a middle schooler's mind in the length of a twenty-minute drive. The conversation somehow meandered from his asking, "What was New Coke?" to "What is health insurance?" to "What is child support?"

Then, just as casually, he asked, "Why *did* you and Dad get divorced?"

That gave me pause because it had never happened before.

Max looked at me expectantly from the passenger seat as my mind whirred through how to handle this. How do you sum up the years of experiences and choices that led to the decision to divorce? You don't want to say anything that reflects poorly on the other parent, or yourself. You don't want to give your child more information than they need, or turn them against the idea of marriage entirely. In the three-second pause it took for all these questions to whiz through my mind, Max grew impatient: "What? You don't even remember?!"

"No, of course I remember!" I replied. "I'm just trying to think how to say it succinctly."

I glanced over and got the "Well, I'm waiting" look.

"Okay. When I was younger, I was always afraid to be honest and speak up when I didn't like something. I just let resentment build up. I started going to therapy and got better about that. I asked Dad to go to therapy with me to work on our marriage, but he wouldn't. Ultimately, since we couldn't fix our problems, we decided to end the marriage and focus on being better parents to you boys."

He nodded, "Understandable."

"The lessons are," I continued—probably unnecessarily, but, you know, Momsplaining—"be honest with people about how you feel. If someone you love asks you to work on a problem, do it. And sometimes leaving a situation is the only way to make things better overall."

I sent him a "How'd I do?" look.

He nodded and said, "Can I put my music on now?"

The lesson? Conversations with your children about the divorce, nesting, and how they are doing, won't be—and shouldn't be—a one-time thing. (And don't take it personally if their only reaction is to tune into their own concerns—at least they know you are there, if and when they do want to talk.)

IN BRIEF: STEP TWO

After you have agreed to nest with your ex, it is time to communicate the plan to your children, together. You should do so openly, but in an age-appropriate ways.

In your initial conversation with your children, you should:
+ Explain what your divorce will mean for them
+ Define nesting and stress that it will allow much of their lives to continue as it has, and they won't need to live in more than one home
+ Remember that *how will this affect me?* is foremost in children's minds when they learn that their parents are divorcing, so focus on answering that question for them

Children of different ages generally react to divorce in different ways:
+ Very young kids may feel confused and not know what to ask
+ Elementary school-age kids often worry that they are the cause of the divorce
+ Middle school-age children and teenagers may feel resentment; at this age they are more capable of articulating their feelings, but they may need to be encouraged to express them

You and your ex will need to have ongoing conversations with each other and your children, especially as you are in the early stages of nesting.

As your children adjust to nesting—and change and mature as they grow older—you should continue to check in with them.

Remember that the emotional well-being and communication abilities of parents influence how well children will handle their own emotions and ability to communicate in their own life—both as children and adults.

CHAPTER 6

Establishing Ground Rules—Step Three

Before we divorced, Bill and I both loved our house and worked together to make it as comfortable and attractive as possible. During the divorce process, we decided it made the most financial sense for Bill to have full ownership of the house. I didn't own the house; I didn't pay rent to him (we'd agreed that the rent I paid on the apartment was a fair contribution to housing costs); yet I lived in the nest half the time.

I was glad that he had responsibility for its care, but I was kind of sad that it wasn't "mine" anymore. To be honest, it wasn't really fair for me to feel this way, since I had agreed to the terms of the settlement. Still, I resented that our house was now Bill's. When he would mention something like an expensive maintenance issue or how the landscaping was getting out of control, I would think to myself, *Well, you wanted the house. It's your problem now.*

Of course, I did basic home care related to my parenting time when I was there: straightening up and quick cleaning, staying on top of the kids and their chores. When I wasn't parenting, I was busy building my freelance writing business. I felt that larger house maintenance issues, like paint touch-up, deep cleaning, lawn care, and landscaping projects were not my responsibility now, especially since it wasn't my house anymore.

But Bill didn't have the time or energy for much beyond the basics of home care, either. The house was starting to show signs of neglect.

It all came to a head when Bill had been away on work travel for almost two weeks. I was writing and trying to meet a tight deadline in the cluttered dining room. The cord on one of the shades was broken and there was a big dent in one of the walls (I was afraid to ask how that happened). I felt a tension headache coming on from the general disarray and disrepair seemingly everywhere I looked. I used to love this room, this house, now I just felt sad—and vaguely annoyed.

I thought I could clear my mind if I got outside for some fresh air while the kids played in the pool. I went out back to open the pool cover and found . . . ick, the water cloudy and a weird color. I texted Bill, SHOULD THE POOL BE GREEN?

I got a one-word reply. (I'll let you use your imagination.)

Bill returned the next day. Almost before he'd set down his bags, we were simultaneously telling the other, "We have to talk."

"The house is looking so in disrepair. It's really stressing me out," I said.

"Caring for the house is really stressing me out," said Bill. "I have to travel for work. If things are neglected, it's just more expensive to fix them."

We decided to revisit our ground rules about house care and financial responsibilities. We agreed that it made sense—since he earns significantly more money than I do—that his job should get more of his focus than weeding the garden or monitoring the pool chemicals. His salary is what gives the kids their education and their home.

But it also did not make sense that I should take on lots more house care responsibilities for free. Bill gets benefits in annual taxes and in the eventual sale of the house that I do not. My giving more of my time to caring for the home makes it a more comfortable place for him and our kids to live. We agreed to financial compensation for the increased home-related tasks I would be taking on.

We also decided to better coordinate efforts on rules for common areas (for example, Bill moved his home office to his bedroom), and have the kids take on additional chores (which they've done more and more through the years as they've gotten older). We'd also plan together in advance which big projects needed to be tackled next, and then how we'd divide the work and the costs.

Again and again, I saw that successful nesting comes back to communication, creativity, and sharing responsibilities. But beyond having in place guidelines for caring for the home, there are other important areas that will benefit from having some established— but capable of evolving—ground rules. Remember: The ultimate goal is that your children and both parents are comfortable and safe in the nest.

When deciding to nest, it's important to define responsibilities and establish some guidelines early on. Some rules will be worked out in your divorce settlement or co-parenting agreement, but oftentimes nesting begins long before couples start the actual divorce process. Putting ground rules down in writing can help you assess if the division of labor and expenses seem fair to both of you.

The areas on which to begin to come to agreement are:

+ Household responsibilities
+ Childcare responsibilities
+ Financial responsibilities (for the nest and children)
+ Tracking expenses

- Communication
- Conduct toward each other

Household Responsibilities

It's important for both of you to come to an agreement on the level of care of the home. If you both are on the same page about that, then—great! But do *you* know a lot of married people who have the same expectations when it comes to what defines a home as "clean" or "organized"? I don't. Ending your marriage probably won't end your different standards or expectations for the home. You should consider these disparities in advance and reach some middle ground, if possible, before they become a source of contention. Yes, this shared space, your home, carries emotional significance. But there's also value in picking your battles. Almost every time I have come into the house, Bill updates me on the state of various things going on and ends by saying, "And the kitchen's clean." And I think, *No, it's not.* But I would never say that out loud. He did all the laundry, the kids are on track with homework, the dog got a lot of playtime, and countless other things were taken care of that I don't always manage to get done myself. It's important to *me* that the kitchen is cleaned a certain way, but in the big scheme of things, it's good enough (until I find time to clean it myself later).

RESPONSIBILITIES TO DISCUSS WITH YOUR EX:

+ Who keeps track of groceries and supplies needed for the household? This may also include at the shared apartment, if applicable.
+ Who will do the shopping for these?
+ Who will be responsible for repair and maintenance, including scheduling service calls, at the home?
+ Who will be responsible for which household chores? On what schedule?
+ Which chores are the children's responsibilities?
+ Who will take care of pet responsibilities, such as walking, grooming, litter-box cleanup, scheduling vet visits?
+ Will you share a car? If so, who will be responsible for its maintenance?

I don't know how common it is, but sharing a car was something that made sense for us for a while. At the time of our divorce, we had a small sedan and a family-sized SUV. When we first divorced, the youngest was still in a booster seat and we were frequently picking up or dropping off various friends of all three kids. Therefore, whoever was in the nest with the kids drove the SUV, whoever was out of the nest drove the Jetta. We had ground rules about the condition of the cars at switchover and returning them with a full tank of gas. Eventually, Bill got a new SUV and I just kept driving the Jetta. We didn't do the weekly switch anymore, but if I needed to use the SUV for transporting groups of kids, he would just let me borrow it as needed.

Childcare Responsibilities

You probably each didn't parent your children exactly the same while you were married, and you don't have to begin to do so now. But there are certain areas that you need to come to agreement on so that the children's needs are met and they have relative consistency in their lives.

RESPONSIBILITIES TO DISCUSS:

+ Who will schedule appointments (doctor, dentist, haircuts, etc.)?
+ Who will take the children to these appointments?
+ Who will stay home with a sick child?
+ What if one of you gets sick—can the other take over parenting?
+ Who is responsible for staying on top of homework?
+ Who will monitor communications, schedule changes, and events from school?
+ How will days off from school be handled—whether they are scheduled or unexpected (like snow days)?
+ Who will arrange for extracurricular activities or classes? And who will drive the children to these?

- Who will arrange for after-school care, babysitting, or summer camps? Who will do the driving?
- Who will plan the children's birthday parties or other social events?
- Which events/special occasions will we both attend?
- How will we divide celebrating holidays? Or will we do some all together?
- How will we handle vacations or trips with the kids? Will each parent trade off or will you plan some that we all do together?

An example of how Bill and I handled scheduling the kids' appointments, like piano lessons or doctor's appointments: Since I worked part time and had a more flexible schedule, I did all the scheduling and most of the driving when the children were younger and couldn't drive themselves. I did the same for grooming and vet appointments for the dog (who never did learn to drive herself). If I had to schedule something during Bill's time, I would check with him and if he couldn't take the child (or dog), then I would do it. It was mostly no big deal for us. But an uneven distribution of that type of labor may quickly become a source of contention for you and your co-parent, especially if you are both working at your jobs the same number of hours or are taking the lead on other responsibilities with the kids.

Financial Responsibilities

As noted at the start of this chapter, a lot of the following may be worked out in your settlement agreement, but it's important to think about these responsibilities early on because it may be a while until you have a formal settlement agreement in place.

Decisions about who pays for what should largely be based on each of your incomes. That's the straightforward way to approach determining what percentage each person contributes to shared expenses. A couple of the nesting families interviewed for this book each make about the same salary, so the co-parents split shared costs evenly. A couple of others have disparate incomes, so each contribute based on their individual incomes, not necessarily the cost of a given item or service.

Then there's me. I was basically a full-time, stay-at-home mom when we divorced. Before moving to Indiana, I had worked in my profession, as a research librarian, full time for over twelve years; then had continued part time in the same profession for almost ten years after that (during which time the three kids were born). When we moved, the youngest was still a baby and Indiana was a heck of a lot cheaper than D.C., so I took the opportunity to stay home full time. The year before our divorce I started my freelance writing work and had a couple of jobs under my belt, but a steady income? Hardly! And what that work brought in—or was likely to bring in any time soon—was minuscule compared to what Bill was making.

We began working with an attorney as soon as we decided to divorce. Based on what I'd made so far and projecting that my workload and income would continue to increase over the next few years, he suggested a small percentage that I would contribute to all shared expenses. Bill and I agreed to that, with the stipulation that when my income went over that estimated amount, we would revisit the agreement and recalculate.

Here's what actually happened, though. Yes, my workload definitely increased—I was really hustling and had a number of clients—but my income was not *substantially* increasing. (Those of you dreaming of that lucrative freelance writing career, take note.) Bill and I began considering if I should I get a full-time job to be able to contribute more financially.

However, there were a couple of issues we encountered as we considered the ramifications of my going back to a full-time job: First, my chosen professions—research librarian and freelance writer—are not as high-paying as Bill's—IT executive. When we decided to have children, we agreed together that it was best for our family if I got off the career advancement path to raise them, and we focused on Bill furthering his career. Even if I could find a full-time job, it would still lag far behind Bill's income. At best, I might be able to adjust my contribution to shared expenses by a few percentage points; that is, not a major difference.

Also, if I began working full time (for not a particularly large financial payoff), what would it cost Bill to hire childcare and house-related care? His travel schedule could be unpredictable, which complicated hiring for help that wasn't consistently required. I was already managing a lot of housekeeping responsibilities in the nest and covering extra hours of childcare so he could focus on work and travel. And he was getting my labor at a pretty good rate.

Ultimately, we agreed that it was of greater value to the well-being of the family, to Bill's career, and to the family's overall financial situation if I continued my flexible freelance writing work and stay-at-home-mom responsibilities.

Ironically, it took our divorce to get both of us to a place of what felt—to me—like, finally, true appreciation for my time and labor as a stay-at-home mom. I now felt comfortable being financially compensated for work I did above and beyond my 50 percent. And Bill was willing to pay for my help for when he couldn't cover his 50 percent.

Our scenario has made me think about the stay-at-home parent who may feel trapped in an unhappy marriage; or, alternately, the high-wage earner who feels they must stay in an unhappy marriage because the other person couldn't make it on their own. The traditional approach to divorce most often is that the stay-at-home parent must find a job and support themselves (and the kids for 50 percent of the time). Who picks up all the work the stay-at-home parent used to do? Might the financials of divorce be configured so that person's labor is valued for as long as the couple agrees it's beneficial to the children and the financial situation of the family? This financial respite postdivorce for the parent who had been focused on child- and home care could also give them more time to pursue a more lucrative career, return gradually to a former profession, or take classes to be ready for a new profession. Or it gives them time to ramp up current income over a reasonable amount of time, as I have done.

Each milestone toward independence for each child—getting a driver's license; jobs, friends, and activities that keep them busy after school and on weekends; going away to college—has allowed me more time to increase my writing work and earning potential. And I still have been fortunate to have spent a lot of time with my kids and working on my home—things I also love to do.

This idea of financial compensation for time and labor above the 50/50 split doesn't only apply to full-time stay-at-home parents. Nester Kate works full time but she had a similar realization when she and her ex divorced. "Monetizing being a wife," she calls it. "I have the 'side hustle' of essentially Airbnb-ing the space in my house to him when he is there for parenting time. He pays me for the time I spend cleaning and shopping. I never minded doing that before, but being financially compensated now negates the resentment I used to feel of being a full-time mom and automatic 'supplier of goods.' And it works for him. He finds it a very easy way to live."

I offer these scenarios for your consideration as you and your partner discuss all the financial aspects of continuing to raise your children together, and putting an initial financial-responsibilities agreement in writing can be your reference point as your situation and your family evolves. Below are suggestions for the financial responsibilities you should consider.

HOUSE-RELATED EXPENSES

What is a new consideration in a nesting divorce is how housing costs will be divided, including for the out-of-the-nest space(s). Depending on your situation and choices, this can be fairly straightforward (many nesters continue to jointly own the home, then split the cost of a shared space, or each may be responsible for all the costs at their own out-of-nest space). We've looked at the different ways our nesting families have arranged their living situation in chapter 3. Chapter 8, on assembling your team, shows how financial and legal professionals can assist you in figuring out what makes the most sense for your situation. But you should begin to consider how the essentials needed for the nest will be paid for.

- Groceries and supplies at the nest, and at the shared space, if applicable
- Mortgage, homeowner's insurance, taxes; rent at a second place, if applicable
- Home repair and emergencies
- Ongoing home maintenance, such as lawn mowing, snow removal
- Replacing worn-out furnishings, linens
- Pet care, including food, toys, vet visits, vaccinations or other medicines, boarding, dog walker

I'd also like to draw attention to the seemingly innocuous topic of groceries. The more nesters I get to know, the more I hear what a source of contention grocery shopping can be. But it's also understandable—as with expectations for how clean the home should be, ideas about food and cooking can be quite different between two parents. Some each do separate shopping for what they will have on hand for themselves and the children when they are on duty. Some nesters have separate shelves in the fridge and pantry that are off-limits to the other parent and the kids. One nester told of leaving a dollar on the counter for her ex because her son drank some of the dad's milk.

Bill and I split groceries 50/50, figuring if we had separate houses, we'd be buying groceries for the kids half of each month.

We each grocery-shop, but (see above about his job and my flexibility) I do about 80 percent of the shopping. We each pay for our own toiletries, but split the cost for what the kids need. Bill and I don't monitor who used more butter (me) or ate the last of the ice cream (Bill). We just figure that kind of stuff "comes out in the wash." We settle who spent how much at the end of the month.

One thing we did have to sort out early on is the occasional splurge on a special meal for the kids. Bill likes to occasionally celebrate the weekend by grilling steaks for the boys. I like to celebrate the weekend by making frozen pizzas. We agreed that, even though we split groceries, it wasn't fair for him to charge me for the steaks, and I don't charge him for my $6.99 gluten-free pizza. We also, of course, don't expect the other parent to contribute if we decide to order in or take the kids out to eat.

CHILD-RELATED EXPENSES

+ Tuition for current schools, if applicable; and/or through college
+ School-related spending, such as laptops or tablets, school supplies, field trips, school lunches, uniforms
+ Extracurriculars, including sports equipment, music or art classes, and instruments or supplies
+ Childcare, such as day care, after-school care, babysitters, summer camps

+ Clothing
+ Medical expenses, including doctor's visits, prescriptions, dentist's visits, orthodontia, health insurance
+ Cars (if you are sharing one with the other parent, or if a kid needs a car): gas, maintenance, repairs, insurance
+ Gifts for your children for birthdays, Christmas, and other holidays, plus gifts the children give to others, such as for friends' birthdays
+ Kids' allowances

Since you are nesting, not much about what is required for the care and raising of children has changed! No second set of clothes for Dad's house, no second set of bedroom furniture at Mom's new place, etc. But you'll still have to either decide what percentage each parent contributes, or, if it makes sense, assigning certain purchases to one parent while the other covers other costs. For example, our kids are covered by Bill's health insurance through his employer; in "exchange" I pay for more of their clothing.

Tracking Expenses

Once you have determined how shared expenses will be split, you need to agree on how expenses will be monitored and settled up between the two of you. Consider the following:

- What method will you use with track expenses?
- How often will expenses be reviewed?
- How soon will payments be made to the other parent?

Most nesters I have spoken with have a shared account to cover home- and family-related expenses with a debit card for each parent. Lauren explains their process when they were still nesting: "When we separated as a couple, we figured out a budget for household expenses. We kept that family account for the household and opened separate accounts for ourselves. When we got paid, we contributed a set amount to the family account and kept whatever was left for personal use. The amount we each contributed was based on salary. I made more money, so I contributed more."

Bill and I have always used a spreadsheet to track spending, each paying for things from our individual accounts or credit cards. I thought we were outliers with our approach, but Karlyn Henry, a Certified Divorce Financial Analyst and Certified Financial Planner in San Jose, California, has worked with many nesting families and reports, "One of my roles is that I help them determine how to manage shared expenses during the transition period and postdivorce. Some people continue [to maintain] joint bank accounts after they separate, but it's also common that each party has their own bank account and pays for things as they come up that they will be reimbursed for later. They keep track on a spreadsheet and settle up every month."

Henry says that in most cases the spreadsheet is a shared document both parents can access to add their expenses. In our case, since 2014 (I don't know why we've never changed this—unless it's that recurring laziness/path of least resistance issue) at the end of each month I email Bill a list of the costs I've covered (for instance, x amount for groceries, x amount for school photos, x amount for dog's vet visit). He plugs my spending into the spreadsheet (which adjusts for percentages we each should be paying), enters his spending that month, then sends me an email with a copy of the spreadsheet and the amount that one or the other of us owes the other person. Our settlement agreement stated that this amount must be paid within two weeks.

Communication

This is a *big* topic, but I'm going to keep it simple for this "ground rules" section. We'll go into the more complicated aspects in chapters 9 and 10 about the trial period and then dealing with problems and changes.

For the early days of nesting, I think there are three ground rules to establish between the two of you to help you communicate effectively:

1. How often will we regularly communicate?

I think a scheduled time once a week is a good idea. It may be tempting to just call or text the other person whenever you have a question or a topic pops into your mind, especially since you probably did ask each other things whenever you randomly felt like it when you were married. But you're not married any more. You need to respect the other person's time, and your own. With a regularly scheduled time to talk, you can pause and ask, "Can this wait for the meeting? Or do I really need an answer right now?" I would bet in most cases, it could wait . . .

Perhaps at first there may be too many changes or new responsibilities to get to everything in a once-a-week meeting. Set up a couple of times a week to talk if you feel this way, but make it the goal to get to one meeting per week. Agree in advance how you will conduct the meeting: in person, on the phone, via video? I prefer in person generally, but sometimes when emotions were too high early in our divorce a phone call was better. Early on, when discussions can quickly turn into arguments, my strongest suggestion is to have your meetings when neither of you is with your children. Bill and I had a local coffee shop where we regularly met—a neutral, public space was helpful to keep us on topic (and prevent emotions from getting too heated).

2. What will we discuss at our regular meetings?

You'll be most productive if you limit yourselves to issues pertaining to the nest, the children, and finances.

This is not the time to get into personal topics, rehash old arguments, or share your personal feelings. Keep these meetings friendly, but strictly business. If any of these topics require more time than you can give it in your regular meeting, agree to another time to give it the attention it deserves.

3. *How will we communicate about things that come up outside of the meetings?*

I mention this because, for a while after our divorce, I was not good at setting boundaries on how we communicated. Big chunks of my day could be lost to texting battles or out-of-the-blue phone calls that turned into an hour-long argument. I thought I was being kind by always taking Bill's calls or responding to his texts, but I was just enabling him to take his anxieties out on me (and I did the same to him). On the other hand, it wasn't effective—and often made the situation worse—if I just ignored his calls or texts. Eventually, I became clearer with Bill about how and when I wanted him to contact me, at what times, and for what reasons; and he became less anxious about everything and better able to deal with situations on his own.

If you can imagine you and your soon-to-be-ex going down the path we did, give some thought to ground rules about communicating to help you both avoid frustration and anxiety.

It can be helpful to establish guidelines for communicating with the children as well. For example:

+ Will there be a set time the kids can expect a call from the non-nest parent each day?
+ Can the kids text or call you whenever they want, or are there restrictions on when they can call (unless it's an emergency)?
+ If the children haven't replied to your call or text within a reasonable time, can you check in with your co-parent?

Conduct Toward Each Other

We'll explore this more in chapters 9 and 10, but consider some initial guidelines about how you will treat each other. This is important especially if you're feeling somewhat contentious toward each other but want to set a good example for your children.

This will take work, as it's probably not something that will come naturally as you are ending your marriage.

+ Don't talk negatively about the other parent to the kids.
+ Be positive in your interactions with each other—co-parenting requires a team approach.
+ Sit together at school functions or other kids' events.
+ Speak kindly of each other in social situations with others.

- Decide in advance which broader family events or other social functions you will both attend (or agree not to attend).

One challenge of nesting co-parenting is that privacy and boundaries can become a source of contention or anxiety. Even if you are not in the home—or the shared apartment—at the same time, if privacy is a concern, you will need to give some forethought to how to protect this.

Christopher Forrest, an attorney and mediator in Fort Wayne, Indiana, recommends establishing private spaces in the shared home for each co-parent that the other won't have access to. "Forbidding the use of monitoring or recording devices could be a consideration, as well," says the attorney.

Forrest also recommends "exclusive access during parenting time"—meaning the other parent cannot show up and expect to be allowed access to the home outside of their parenting time.

Nester Michael explains he and his ex always text each other if one of them is going to come into the house while the other is on parenting duty, but not at home. "Early on, I did need to make clear the boundaries on my time at the house," he says "For example, she would come in early to put groceries away before her parenting time began, but her arrival was disruptive to my time with the kids.

We have found it works better to make those transitions as quick as possible."

As for dates or romantic partners in the space? As discussed in chapter 4, this can lead to some fiery exchanges and drama if ground rules haven't been established.

Nester Lauren describes her approach: "While we shared the sublet apartment, our main agreement was that we wouldn't allow any new partners to sleep over there. We had the same agreement for the nest. Eventually, we agreed that my new partner was welcome in the nest, except for sleepovers."

Putting the Plan into Action

Establishing the ground rules is essential to launching nesting as smoothly as possible. If you are planning to meet with a lawyer or mediator soon, draft your ground rules and use them for a trial run. This will give you an idea of how nesting will realistically work for your family. If you discover sticking points that you cannot sort out yourselves, then this third party can help as you prepare your formal agreement. We'll look at this process more closely in chapter 8, "Assembling Your Team—Step Five."

Be aware, and understanding, that the day-to-day implementation of your rules may need to be adjusted to best respond to the circumstances—some days with children are just more challenging than others. You may also determine that you agree on the end goal of a rule (for example, "Kids do their homework every night"), but exactly how that is implemented may vary between parents.

For Bill and me, some rules were consistent and easy to monitor because we were nesting. Morning and bedtime routines were almost identical. The kids always put their backpacks and homework in the same place, no matter which parent was there, and did their homework at the same locations (dining room table for the older two, kitchen table for the youngest). We had agreed-upon locations where phones and iPads had to be placed before bedtime; that is, *not* in their bedrooms.

But some rules varied between us, too. Bill was big on the kids getting their homework done before any screen time; I didn't mind if they had some screen time to unwind right after school, as long as they had all their homework done an hour before their bedtime. They knew the rules were different, but they also knew we both were paying attention to homework.

There is something to be said for not getting too bogged down in spelling out every detail. Use your knowledge of yourself, your children, and the other parent, and choose what you feel are the essential areas to address from the start.

After all that's been outlined in this chapter, though, I would be remiss not to leave you with these words of wisdom from our nester Kate: "Early on, we had a very comprehensive parenting plan. But eventually I realized it wasn't a reference point for anyone but me. We've just been winging it ever since. Everything works out fine and I'm a lot more relaxed."

IN BRIEF: STEP THREE

Essential to a successful—and sustainable—launch of nesting is establishing agreed-upon ground rules between both parents. These include:

- Household responsibilities: What are the agreed-upon responsibilities to maintain the home (and an out-of-nest living space, if applicable)? What housekeeping standards can we agree to? Who is responsible for doing what?
- Childcare responsibilities: What is required to continue the standard of care we've established for our children? Who will handle which responsibilities?
- Financial responsibilities: Who pays for what? Determine the appropriate contributions, based on salaries and in-the-nest parenting time.
- Consider the value of "unpaid" time and labor toward the good of the family and how to adjust for that financially beyond a standard 50/50 split. Could some of the extra time and labor invested in caring for children and the nest factor into how expenses are configured?

Effective ground rules address more than simple logistics of who pays for what and who is responsible for which tasks. When setting ground rules be sure to place particular emphasis on how to:

+ Communicate respectfully with each other in front of the children
+ Maintain appropriate conduct toward each other, with an emphasis on privacy and boundaries
+ Coordinate with each other and be consistent with how each of you communicates with the children

When establishing ground rules, expect that there may be some changes that require flexibility, and that some may become less important over time as you settle into the day-to-day specifics of nesting. Have regular meetings with your ex to assess whether any ground rules need to change.

CHAPTER 7

Telling Family and Friends—Step Four

I t may be difficult to break the news about your divorce to the people in your lives. Will they be judgmental, worried, exceedingly curious, surprised, or—this may even be worse—*not* surprised? Also, telling people that you are nesting—which more often than not requires explaining what *that* means—adds another layer of confusion. You should expect a variety of reactions from people when you tell them about your divorce and nesting—and prepare yourself to address their curiosity in ways with which *you* are comfortable.

Lauren, our nester in Brooklyn, says there are occasions when people have responded in ways that make her uneasy: "They say 'I could never do that!' or 'Isn't that weird to still be around your ex?'"

Not surprising, since many people are uncomfortable with scenarios that are out of the ordinary. Maybe someday people will think it's weird that parents used to divorce and make their kids do all the work of moving back and forth between two houses; but, for now, we nesters are the weirdos.

The good news is that many nesters have found that reactions from others are mostly positive. As nester Kate in Toronto says, "People are fascinated and want to know more. Mostly, when I tell others about nesting, they are just wowed and say, 'What a gift you're giving your children!'"

Still, it can be intimidating or embarrassing to tell other people you are getting divorced. Will others judge you, see your marriage as a failure, or want to know more details than you are willing to share?

So, my first word of advice is to have a plan. Before you and your ex tell the people in your life about your divorce and nesting arrangement, it's important to get your story straight, together. That doesn't necessarily mean sugarcoating the news; it is a divorce after all.

Your Divorce Story

You probably heard the old adage, "There are three sides to every story: your side, my side, and the truth."

It can be tempting to want everyone to know *your* side of your divorce in hopes of garnering sympathy and support. But it will likely serve you better (and your ex, your kids, your friends, and your family) if some of the details of your divorce are kept private—between you and your ex, you and your therapist, and/or you and only your very closest friends.

When you're in the high-emotions stage of divorce, it may be difficult to take the ten-thousand-foot view on why you got divorced and to understand the roles both of you played in the demise of your romantic partnership. It's human nature to focus on what egregious things happened to you most recently and want to let others know the challenges you are facing. It's also human nature for other people to remember the bad things you tell them about your ex more than the good—those make the better stories, right? But most people don't need to know very much about your divorce. This is especially true if you are hoping to move successfully into nesting. Friends and family will likely continue to be around your ex and your children for years to come and the more positive—or at least neutral—they can be about your ex and your divorce, the easier it will be for all of you.

That's why it's important to have an agreed-upon version of your divorce story that is acceptable for public consumption. In our case, Bill and I agreed that, for most people, we would present something along the lines of what I call "the celebrity publicist's template": "Despite trying to fix our problems for years, we have grown apart and agree it's best to end our marriage so we can focus on being the best parents possible to our kids." (We didn't have to add "Please respect our privacy at this time" because we're not famous and generally don't have problems being hounded by paparazzi.) Boil it down to the basics and save the epic tales for your therapist.

Your basic script can be simply to state: "We're divorced." (Or "We're getting divorced" or "separating" or "no longer partners"— whichever is most comfortable for you.)

Then—depending on who's asking (more on that later)—you can choose to briefly go into how you both are doing, and/or how the kids are doing; for instance, "We're both fine, thanks." "Yes, the kids are handling things well."

Inquiring Minds Want to Know About Nesting

Part of the challenge in explaining nesting to others is that you're not only telling them about a significant change in your family, you're also indirectly offering your own critical view of what typically happens in divorce by doing something entirely different! You don't always need to mention that, but when you do, it will take more than a few words to describe. Early on, I developed my "elevator pitch." As with the divorce, the more succinctly I state it—hand gestures help!—the easier it is for others to digest:

"Our living arrangement's kind of unusual. The boys stay in the house [*hands together in front of me, fingertips touching like I'm holding a big snowball*] and their dad and I have separate places [*right hand out, then in again, as left hand moves out*] where we live outside the nest. We move in and out to take care of them" [*hands back in front, holding the snowball*]."

Some people like to use the "baby birds in a nest" analogy. Another way to explain it is that you're giving your children custody of the home, which is likely to be met with a chuckle. Regardless of how you explain nesting, it's important to stress that it is a child-centered approach to divorce and co-parenting, and a decision that you and your ex arrived at together.

The other factor to consider when telling others about your divorce and nesting is who exactly is receiving the news. This often determines how you should frame it—and even how much you tell that person.

GENERAL ACQUAINTANCES

For almost every general acquaintance, a basic script about your divorce more than suffices, but not always. Even though I had prepared myself to share our divorce news with friends and family, I was not ready—which is why I'm giving you a heads-up!—for the number of times I found myself having to tell people who weren't friends about my divorce. You know, those people that you kind of know: friends of friends you've met a few times, teachers or other parents you know from school, friends of your parents. You know, the kind of people you make casual chitchat with if you run into them at the grocery store. The kind of acquaintances who know you just well enough to ask, "Is your husband still traveling so much for work?" or "Will you both be at the school fund-raiser again this year?" I guess you could just be very vague in your answers . . . but I felt a quick "Actually, we got divorced" response was honest and to the point.

Also, and this may be just because of the smallish town I live in, I was surprised to find that I did have to explain the situation to my tree guy and the exterminator at different times because they had heard about our divorce and nesting from other clients. I don't talk to them in person very often, but when I do, they still—years later—very nicely ask if we're still "doing that thing, with the kids?" and tell me how cool they think it is. Validation can come from unexpected people!

With general acquaintances, you will likely find that some are more curious than others—especially if you mention nesting. Bill and I agree that the most frequent questions are:

+ Isn't that expensive?
+ How do you date?
+ How long will you do it?
+ Why didn't you just stay married?/Isn't that just like still being married?

The average casual acquaintance doesn't need to hear a deep dive into my thoughts and reasoning, so I think the more succinct the answer, the better:

Isn't that expensive?
"No. We found it was cheaper than buying or renting a second place that could fit our kids and keep them close to their school."

How do you date?
"We have time to date when we are not in the nest on parenting duty."

How long will you do it?
"Until it no longer makes sense for us."

Why didn't you just stay married?
"It was best for us to divorce."

Of course, if a casual acquaintance keeps prodding for more than you are willing to share, you have no obligation to tell them more. I've found laughing off an unwanted question with a head shake and then changing the topic back to them (people love to talk about themselves!) tends to do the trick.

SHARED FRIENDS AND FAMILY

Beyond general acquaintances, there is your broader circle of good friends and family you want to inform about this big change in your lives—the type of people you would feel bad if they just heard the news from somebody else.

Bill and I agreed that, after we told our children, we wanted—together—to let our group of family and close friends know. That was a group of thirty or so people. We talked it over and decided that a group email would be a good way to spread the word. It was quicker than calling or emailing each and every one of them. We also had a lot of shared friends and we felt better about the news coming from both of us rather than seeming like we were sorting them into "my side"/"your side." You could do a blind cc, but we sent it so everyone could see who had been told—hoping to keep people from wondering, *Did they tell so-and-so, or should I give them a call?*

We opened a bottle of Dom Perignon we'd received from Bill's brother-in-law as a wedding present (which was still fantastic after all these years) and together wrote what we hoped was a clear message that, even though we were divorcing, we still cared about each other, and we still wanted all of them to be in both of our lives and the lives of our children. We explained that we would be nesting and told people that they were welcome to stay at our home any time. And we attached a picture, taken by our oldest son, of us toasting our divorce to show everyone that we were still quite amicable. (Or at least amicable enough to share a bottle of Dom together!)

After that email, a number of people reached out to connect and the support we got back was heartwarming.

Michael and his ex did a similar thing (I forgot to ask if they drank champagne, too): "After telling family and close friends, we did a joint Facebook post, for people who didn't already know. In that post we explained that we were nesting. Everyone was super supportive and thought nesting was a great idea."

Jean says that she and Tedd took a less coordinated approach: "Our list of shared friends was long. We didn't announce it, just told people one by one and let it spread."

YOUR INDIVIDUAL CLOSE FRIENDS AND FAMILY

Your spouse may know these people, but you have the primary close relationship with them—your best friends from college, childhood friends, favorite cousin, for example. They know you well, but they may not be as immersed in your daily life as other friends and family. For me, these were the people who—even though we'd included them in the group email—I felt deserved a phone call to answer their questions, go into more detail about how I was doing, and more fully explain nesting and how the kids were doing. I remember having a list and just tackling a call a day every time I was out of the nest and at the apartment. It took a couple of weeks. It felt kind of weird at first—probably for them, too—but it reconnected us, and some of these people I've become much closer to since the divorce.

Then there are the very close friends and family you've already looped in on your marriage issues, perhaps for years. Really close friends like that will always side with you, as they should. As you move into nesting you may ask them not to bring up all the negative things you said about your ex in the past. But you don't want them to forget, either—sometimes you just need to vent to someone who has heard it all.

I asked licensed counselor Réa Wright how best to explain to them your divorce and your decision to nest and to ask for their support. She says, "First off, it's nobody's damn business, and that includes parents and siblings. Sometimes when you communicate with family, parents particularly, it can come across less about you telling them what's going on and more about your asking their permission. Family members may feel you are opening the door for them to tell you that you shouldn't get divorced."

I hadn't ever brought up our marital issues with my parents and sister—my family members we saw the most—out of embarrassment, maybe, or just not feeling close enough to share that kind of information. I probably wouldn't have told them anything until we actually decided to divorce, but my therapist advised otherwise. She knew Bill and I were considering divorce and sometimes things were getting fairly contentious between us. Since my parents and my sister lived in the same town, and our kids were comfortable spending time with them, my therapist suggested that I loop them in and explain that Bill and I were having a "rough patch." They didn't need to know all the specifics, just that I might need their help with the kids on short notice. That really was excellent advice. It made me feel more comfortable about asking for their help with the kids when I did need it; and it gave them a chance to mentally prepare themselves before I told them we were definitely moving ahead with the divorce. You may want to consider the same approach if you have a very good friend or family members in town, who could be on call should you need it.

BARELY ACQUAINTANCES/STRANGERS WHO ARE DIVORCED

More rarely—but often enough that I'm warning you—I get rather odd reactions from people I barely know. I'm caught off guard because I may not even know that the other person has been divorced and/or what their co-parenting arrangement was. Then I wonder if my mentioning nesting comes across as a criticism of their choices—which was not my intent at all.

"Our divorce must have been a lot worse than yours."

"You're lucky—we could never have done that."

"Your ex must be a lot cooler than mine."

I must admit, the first few times I got these types of responses, it bugged me a bit. Those are kind of presumptuous things to say, right? That my divorce was easy? That I just lucked into this nesting situation? I wouldn't presume to comment on their divorce. Why were they being rather dismissive of mine? It occurred to me recently that maybe I should stop taking it personally. Perhaps my describing nesting sounded like a criticism of what they did (it wasn't, I swear). Or maybe they have regrets about how things happened and how their kids were impacted. Maybe they really did have a truly awful, ugly divorce. Divorce is hard. Figuring out co-parenting is hard.

So now, when I get these types of comments, I just try to nod and smile in a supportive way and say, "Divorce is hard."

Except for that "Your ex must be a lot cooler than mine."

To that I say, "Have you *met my ex*?"

Create Some Boundaries When They're Needed

Most likely, as you begin to tell your divorce story to others, you'll quickly realize who you can trust, who will just listen, and who will think you are looking to them for advice. It's up to you to determine what you personally need most at that time and who are the best people to talk with.

Nester Suzanne concurs: "So many people have advice for you when you're getting divorced. The traditional divorce stories so often come from people being scared or heartbroken. So some people feel free to tell you that divorce is a bad idea, or that they know someone who tried nesting and it didn't go well."

I love her advice: "You have to have a pretty strong inner compass, trusting that you know what you are doing is right for you and your family."

If you are this far down the path into nesting, you have obviously given the matter a lot of thought and have strong reasons for your decisions. It's completely reasonable for you to be a little forceful, if needed, about the fact that a decision has been made and you're not looking for advice.

As nester Jean says, "For us, we made clear it was *our* decision. We ran the idea of nesting by a couple of close friends for feedback, but we weren't asking their permission."

If close friends and family are pushing for more details or to give you their opinion, counselor Wright advises, "You could say, 'If you need more information, you can ask and I will answer as much as I feel comfortable.' But it's okay to set boundaries. They may not like that you are getting divorced or may not understand why you are nesting. You can say, 'This is what we as a couple have decided to do and we'd like you to support us. Our entire focus is on making this as loving and safe as possible for the kids.'"

Some people, even people very close to you, don't want to hear about the good things that have come out of your divorce. They don't want to hear about your satisfaction that you are divorced or your happiness about the success of nesting. They prefer to hear you bad-mouth your ex, or stay sad that you're divorced, or vent about your struggles with nesting. I'm not a therapist—though, Lord knows, I've talked to enough of them—but I *think* this, again, is not really about you, but about them. Perhaps they are not happy, so they don't want you to be happy.

At first, when I got leading questions, like "Is Bill still getting so angry?" or "Do your kids still need to see a therapist?" I would find myself over-explaining or defending myself. Or, if my defenses were down, I'd get dragged into a complaining session, and then I'd be in a bad mood for the rest of the day.

It may surprise you which friends or family members won't be there in the way you'd hoped. Depending on the person and your relationship with them, you can point out to them what they are doing and ask them to stop, or you can decide to just change the topic when they try to turn positive things you say (such as "Bill and I have been getting along pretty well lately" or "The kids are handling the divorce really well") in a negative direction.

There are also the people who just feel uncertain or uncomfortable about your decision. They aren't opposed exactly, just maybe feeling awkward about your divorce ("How am I supposed to act toward your ex?") or unclear about how nesting could work and or how they will explain it to other people ("What are we supposed to put in the Christmas letter?"). Suzanne recalls, "Our families, who have really been great overall, had some issues in the beginning. One parent or another would ask, 'Well, what am I supposed to tell people?' They probably would have preferred not to have to explain it at all."

People who know you both well may still be biased since they've also grown up in the "pick a side" divorce culture. And people who don't know you well likely have no idea what to think—just that it's not "normal." I can recall early post-divorce casual social get-togethers—like neighborhood barbecues or functions at school for parents—when a friend would tense up if talking to one of us and the other strolled up to join the conversation. Perhaps they were wondering, *Are they really okay with this or are they going to start fighting—or crying!—in front of me!?* The first few birthday parties for our kids, at least one family member would nervously ask, "You're *both* going to be there?" Perhaps thinking, *That will make me feel awkward because it is weird.* And it took a couple of years before friends and family who used to visit regularly from out of town would come to stay with us again. Maybe wondering, *What will it be like to be in their house like old times, but now they're divorced?* Their reluctance and dubiousness understandably stems from the fact that it is very rare for divorced people to find a way to get along and, also, still stay in each other's lives.

I do think Bill and I, in our zeal to stay connected to people we cared about, may have tried to force interactions before others had accepted our divorce or understood how nesting could work for us. I can recall inviting friends who were couples over to the nest early on in the hopes of friendships continuing as they had before the divorce. Bill and I thought we were acting like our usual selves, but our friends definitely did not seem relaxed, and no longer reciprocated by inviting both of us to their homes. I recall several occasions where a friend would check with me about which of us to invite to a social occasion. Even though I would tell them it was okay to invite both of us, that rarely happened. In hindsight, maybe Bill and I were not acting as normally as we thought, maybe our efforts to make our friends comfortable were actually making them uncomfortable. A big life change like divorce can leave you reeling. Even if you are certain that you appear just fine, there can be an unbalancedness that others pick up on. Perhaps we should have been less selfishly focused on keeping things the same with our friends, and been more understanding that they might need time to process our divorce and grow comfortable around us again on their own.

I'm not sure it that would have been the best approach, or not. But I guess my point is that not only do you need to be gentle with yourself, but also with those who care for you. Give them some time to adjust to the situation as well.

The good news is that most of the people in your life do want to be supportive, but may need suggestions for simple and practical ways to do so. When you feel secure in your decision to end your marriage and to nest for the good of your kids, you can confidently ask others for help when and if you need it. Wright suggests how to approach asking others to help you: "Have specific suggestions for what help you need from them or give them ideas for how to help you. If you don't yet know exactly what you need, tell them that you will let them know as you figure it out."

Sometimes just telling people how much you appreciate their love and support, just knowing that they are there for you if you need them is enough. This gives both of you the time and emotional space to figure out how to navigate a changed relationship and keep your friendship going.

IN BRIEF: STEP FOUR

Telling others that your marriage has ended—and that you are going to nest!—can feel intimidating. Will people be disappointed, surprised, or judgmental? Will you feel supported or embarrassed? And whom do you tell, and how much, and when?

Breaking the process into steps and being prepared can help you get through it. Most of all, it's important to be secure in your own well-thought-out decision to nest and your commitment to putting your children first.

When preparing to tell others about your divorce and plans to nest, you should:

- ✦ Come up with a "for public consumption" story of your divorce that both of you will use, and be prepared with succinct answers for general acquaintances
- ✦ Consider informing mutual friends and family together
- ✦ Realize that explaining nesting may take some extra effort, so be prepared for the most common questions:
  - ▪ Isn't that expensive?
  - ▪ How do you date?

- How long will you do it?
- Why didn't you just stay married?/Isn't that just like still being married?
+ Accept that there may be disappointing reactions, or unhelpful advice from friends and family. It's important to recognize that those reactions may have more to do with their own issues with a partner or marriage than with what you are going through

You should also give some thought in advance about help you need or would appreciate from family and friends—and ask for it. You can ask for practical help, like babysitting or carpooling. You can also remind loved ones that what you want most from them is emotional help; sometimes you may just need a person you are close with to listen and provide unconditional support in your decision to end your marriage and choose nesting.

Don't be afraid to create boundaries when they are needed. It's up to you to determine what you personally need most from everyone in your life, and who will be able to provide the emotional support you and your family need as you all adjust to these changes in your life.

CHAPTER 8

Assembling Your Team: Legal, Financial, Mind and Body, Practical Help—Step Five

The most important ventures in life often require help from others—and divorce and nesting are certainly no exception. One of the appeals of this approach to co-parenting is that it allows much of the status quo of your family life to remain. Still, because your marriage is ending, there may be a switching of gears on your shared vision for the future. You may need, or want, to reenvision your goals for your family and reassess your financial situation and how those goals can best be achieved.

There are plenty of resources, both print and online, to help navigate the ins and outs of divorce, from the financial to the legal to the emotional (see "Further Reading and Resources" for some suggestions). Rather than attempting to distill all that information, this chapter will look at nesting-specific concerns you and the professionals with whom you are working should consider as you move forward with your plan.

Financial and Legal Help

First, a disclaimer: While the professionals in this section are incredibly knowledgeable about the finances and legalities of divorce and nesting, their insights may not reflect the laws where you live. Professionals in your local area can best answer your specific questions and describe how their services can meet your needs.

That said, every couple who hopes to nest should consider two main questions that will undoubtedly shape their financial plans and legal agreement:

+ Do you and your ex want to change the current ownership of the family home?
+ Are you officially divorcing as soon as possible, or working toward divorcing in the near future?

THE FAMILY HOME

One of the appeals of nesting is continuing ownership of the family home, most often for personal reasons (like continuity for the children) but also quite often for the financial benefits of not having to purchase a second home.

Nester Michael and his ex-wife are both teachers and bought their house during the recession when real estate was more reasonably priced in their area of northern Virginia. "We couldn't afford our current house now," says Michael. "If we'd sold the house, neither of us could have found anything nearly as nice in the school zone. We see a lot of benefit in continuing to share the ownership going forward."

Many nesters continue to jointly own the home, as Tedd and Jean, Michael and his ex, and Suzanne and her ex do. Kate began nesting several years after she and her ex ended their marriage. She moved from the family home to a new place after their split and that is now the home in which they nest. Lauren and her ex jointly owned their co-op until they decided recently to end nesting and put it on the market. In my case, when Bill and I divorced, he took over full ownership of the house and I took a financial payout as part of our settlement agreement.

There is no right answer to how you and your ex continue to own the home after your divorce. If you are exploring the pros and cons or thinking about changing the ownership agreement, a Realtor or a financial professional could be helpful in figuring out the specifics of how best to do that. See more on that in Financial Team on the next page.

DIVORCE TIMING

Not everyone who ends their marriage immediately divorces (as discussed in chapter 4, "Agreeing to Nest with Your Spouse/Soon-to-Be-Ex—Step One"). Of the nesters described in this book, Bill and I and Michael and his ex were the only ones who actually went through the divorce process at the same time as we were establishing the nesting situation. As a couple, it's also perfectly reasonable to establish that your romantic partnership is over, but determine a different timeline for your divorce: Suzanne and her ex waited several years until her ex wanted to remarry; Tedd and Jean divorced after they stopped nesting, for example. Lauren and her partner didn't need to deal with the process of divorce, as gay marriage was not yet legal in New York when they started their family together. Whatever you decide to do, it can be beneficial to consult with a professional to think through the legal issues of divorce, especially as they relate to nesting after divorce. It is also a good idea to loop in your financial professional— or begin working with one—to help you prepare for the financial changes that ending your romantic partnership may bring.

FINANCIAL TEAM

You may feel that you have a handle on all the financial aspects of your divorce and nesting. That's great. Nesting allows continuity of family finances from marriage through separation and divorce. Many nesters continue with the same approach to finances, especially in the early stages. Depending on your circumstances, there may be other professionals who you would wish to consult, such as a tax accountant or an estate planning attorney. Also, if you are pursuing divorce immediately, the attorney or mediator will be advising you about certain financial matters and can work cooperatively with your financial professionals.

If you don't already have relationships with financial professionals, personal connections can be an excellent source of referrals. "Of course people you know who are successful with their money management can connect you with their advisers," says Ron Carboni, a financial planner in Fort Wayne, Indiana.

If you already work with a financial professional, they can also be helpful in finding other professionals. Karlyn Henry, a Certified Divorce Financial Analyst (CDFA) in San Jose, California, says that "divorce financial planners frequently work in concert with family attorneys, CPAs, and Realtors, and can absolutely refer clients to other professionals."

If you are divorcing at this time, you may be wondering if you should begin working with your own professional, rather than continuing to share that person with your ex. If you are concerned about confidentiality, financial planner Carboni suggests, "A reputable professional wouldn't share one client's financial information with an ex-spouse. The adviser should stay neutral and work for both sides. But the most important thing is that you like working with the person." He notes that you may wish to stay with the same firm but choose another adviser there to personally work with. If that makes you uncomfortable, then searching for your own adviser or firm is certainly reasonable. You could continue to work with the same person as your ex in the interim.

Since the value—and costs—of the family home can be a large factor in many of the financial arrangements involved in nesting, you may want to speak with a local Realtor to make sure you understand your situation. Deborah Lansing, a Realtor in Montclair, New Jersey, says, "Your home is a financial investment. A Realtor can help you evaluate your return on investment—the financial benefits, or downsides, of holding on to the house. My role is being able to interpret the market and assess where it might be going."

If you have decided to nest, a Realtor can help you explore rental or purchase options in your area as well. Also, if you are considering renovating your home to allow for nesting, as our nester Suzanne did, Lansing says, "A Realtor can look at the design of the house and explain what additions or changes tend to be most valued in terms of eventual resale. They also can help people think through the financial scenarios—for example, would one person pay the mortgage while the other pays for the renovations, and how might that affect the eventual sale proceeds? A Realtor can also put clients in touch with contractors and mortgage people they trust."

HELPING YOUR TEAM HELP YOU

When you meet to discuss nesting and divorce with your financial adviser, come prepared with:

+ your thoughts on home ownership
+ information on your divorce timeline (if you have one)
+ and your goals for nesting.

The financial aspects you outlined in your ground rules (see chapter 6) can be a helpful starting point for your discussion with an adviser. Certified Divorce Financial Analyst Henry also suggests that, if you are meeting with a new professional for the first time, you should provide them with as much information as possible about your income and assets. Henry says a CDFA can then "help nesting clients with creating a spending plan that considers housing costs such as reasonable house maintenance costs as well as childcare and other shared costs, based on the client's financial situation."

This would also be the time to discuss any expected job changes for either parent that might affect the family's financial situation, as well as if and how one parent could be financially compensated for additional time and labor taken on because of your nesting agreement.

NESTING-SPECIFIC QUESTIONS FOR THE FINANCIAL

TEAM MEMBER:

✦ What makes the most financial sense for ownership of the nest?

✦ What might be the financial considerations when we eventually sell the nest? (For example, tax implications, costs of preparing the home for sale, and then selling the home.)

✦ What would be reasonable percentages for each of us to contribute to shared nesting-related costs (including major expenses and emergencies)?

✦ What might alimony or child support look like, based on our incomes and the finances of the nesting situation?

✦ What changes to our wills or life insurance policies might be required, in light of nesting, to provide for the care of our children and/or the other parent?

Carboni makes an important point, "Not every kid is ready to be independent at eighteen, or even right after college. Sometimes parents find themselves providing for their kids longer than they thought they might be." (We look at this and how it relates to nesting in chapter 10, "Down the Road: Changes, Challenges, Growth, and Transitioning Out of Nesting.") You may want to consider and discuss the following with your financial adviser:

- Will we really want to sell the nest as soon as the last child leaves for college—or might we want them to still be able to "come home?"
- What if one of the children has issues—physical, mental, or financial—that may impact their ability to be independent by a certain age? Will we continue to nest or work together in some other way to help support them?

Henry, the Certified Divorce Financial Analyst, says, "There are laws the parties could follow and fall back on, of course, but a divorce financial planner's main goal is to meet the family's needs creatively, helping them make educated financial decisions for the good of all of their futures."

LEGAL TEAM

If you are considering nesting, you are likely not attracted to the idea of a contentious, drawn-out, and expensive divorce. Despite the stereotypes of the cutthroat divorce attorney, there are many attorneys and mediators who focus on collaborative, quick, and relatively painless divorces for their clients. But don't be deterred if it takes a couple of tries to find a professional with whom you are comfortable and who will support you in your plans to nest. While every attorney may not have direct experience with nesting co-parenting, most should at least be familiar with the concept as "nesting is increasingly being established by the courts on a temporary basis until a final parenting plan is created and each party has found suitable living arrangements," according to Jill Brakeman, a family attorney and mediator in Litchfield, Connecticut.

As discussed above, referrals from people you respect can be an excellent way to connect with the right legal professional. Whether or not the attorney has set up a nesting arrangement before may be less important than if you feel comfortable communicating with them and find them supportive of your goals.

It may take more than one attempt to find the right legal professional. Nester Michael describes his first attempt at finding an attorney: "I met with her for a very expensive hour and a half of Zoom calls. When I asked her, 'We're considering nesting. Where do we go from here?' She said, 'I think you're insane and that's a terrible idea.'"

Fortunately, he and his ex had better luck with a mediator, who was referred to them by a friend: "She was familiar with nesting, though she hadn't yet seen anyone make it work. But she was willing to help us figure out our nesting agreement and craft a separation agreement that respected nesting. She knew how to write an agreement that would be easy for a judge to understand."

Of course, you want to work with someone who is supportive of your goals (if not, don't hire them), but questions and concerns about your proposal are not necessarily a red flag that this person is wrong for you. Brakeman explains, "A good mediator will bring all the pros and cons to the table for the parties to take into consideration in determining whether a nesting arrangement is truly in the children's best interest." The question is this: Do you feel they are listening to you and willing to do whatever they can to help you reach your goal?

PREPARING—HELPING YOUR TEAM HELP YOU

You already have valuable information to help guide your legal professionals since you have made it here to step five, agreeing to give nesting a try and setting up some ground rules. The specifics of your nesting agreement and ground rules may evolve as you work with your legal professional, but use the work you have done so far to help these professionals do their best for you. Explain to them the nesting situation you envision and share with them the ground rules you have established at this point, especially any ground rules or issues that are not working as well as you had hoped. Any financial information related to the nesting arrangement or the overall state of your finances—especially if you have information to share from meeting with your financial team member (see above)—will help them understand how to craft an appropriate agreement. Disparities in income (if any) and whether one parent will be compensated for nesting-related labor should also be discussed.

Attorneys and mediators will be most comfortable working with you if they see that you are committed to nesting and have given some thought to the scenario you envision. They also will be most supportive if there is evidence of good communication and emotional maturity on the part of both parents. Attorney and mediator Brakeman says, "The parents need to have a strong co-parenting relationship to avoid conflicts in the shared living arrangements. The parties will also need good communication, not only as it pertains to parenting, but also to financials if they are sharing residence costs. A nesting agreement in a family where there is high conflict can make the children's environment worse, not better. Clear drafting of all legal documents and careful consideration of the family financials, as well as working with a mental health professional, are effective ways to help avoid problems.

Share the ground rules you have already established with your team members, which are a strong starting point to developing an appropriate settlement.

NESTING-SPECIFIC QUESTIONS FOR THE LEGAL TEAM MEMBER:

A good legal professional will have these concerns on their radar already, but you should come prepared to ask how the following nesting-specific issues will be addressed in the settlement:

- How do parenting-time percentages relate to time in the nest (i.e., is there a set transition time on a set day)?
- Do we want to establish any rules about access to the home when the other parent is on parenting duty? Any rules about private space within the home?
- How should we continue home ownership and split financial responsibility for it (including shared household expenses, utilities, maintenance, and emergency repairs)?
- How will the out-of-nest residence(s) be paid for?
- How should we divide other nesting-related shared expenses?
- How, or will, nesting-related expenses affect a child support order?

YOU MAY ALSO WANT TO ASK YOUR ATTORNEY OR MEDIATOR:

- Do they have any concerns about the case going to a judge who is not familiar with nesting? If so, how would they, the legal professional, prepare for that?

In 2014, nesting was practically unheard of in Fort Wayne when I approached my attorney, Christopher Forrest, with the idea. He recalls, "I wanted to accomplish what you wanted, but I was concerned about presenting something 'outside of the box' to the court." He says now, however, judges are more familiar with the concept as nesting is becoming more commonly used as a transition toward the two-home approach. While longer-term nesting is still rare, Forrest and the other attorneys and mediators I spoke with all agree that judges are most supportive of clear plans that show cooperation between the parents in the best interest of the kids. "There's not much you can't resolve without creativity in a collaborative process," attorney and mediator Brakeman says. "If the goal is to nest, judges will support whatever is best for the kids and what the parents want to make happen."

Even if you are considering nesting for an indeterminate period of time, your legal professional may advise, for the ease of the court's understanding or for other reasons, that nesting be presented as a trial run that can be revisited by the parents (see more on that in chapter 9, "The Trial Period—Step Six"). Susan Guthrie, an attorney and mediator in Chicago, says, "A parent should check in with their attorney on the feasibility of setting up a nesting plan on a trial basis to see how it will work for the family. There will be issues that need to be addressed during the trial and it is best to do this ahead of time, when possible."

Forrest suggested creating a plan that can be reviewed over time, "a side agreement, a 'joint parenting plan' that can be changed without going to the court. Depending on the parties, they could do it on their own, or they could have help from the attorney or mediator to create a template."

It's also important to discuss considerations for when—and how—nesting will eventually end, even if you don't have a specific end date in mind at this time.

Michael recalls, "Our mediator encouraged us to include some concrete provisions in our agreement to serve as legal backup if we decide at some point that nesting isn't working. She made a big deal about having multiple backup plans. At times that was tough because we were discussing scenarios that might not even happen. But, in the long run, it's pretty clearly spelled out."

I remember having a few back-and-forths with my attorney about how nesting might end, especially since Bill had full ownership of the home. I didn't *want* to talk about nesting ending while I was working so hard on starting it, but attorneys like mine often view this as essential. "I wanted there to be protection so that you couldn't just be kicked out of the house on a day's notice," says Forrest. "But I also wanted to avoid either of you being stuck in a nesting situation for too long if you wanted to get out of it—because that would just create more problems. We needed clarity on how it *could* end."

As an example, in our case, we agreed there must be thirty days' notice given to the other parent before nesting could end; also, should Bill decide to sell the house, I was given the "right of first refusal" on the offer he received.

Practical Help Team

While it is true that nesting will provide more consistency in your children's daily lives, *you* may find that daily life is not as consistent as it used to be. Though you are still parenting in your home, you are no longer parenting with another adult around to help. Being a single parent is challenging, even if you are nesting.

Consider whether there may be other people or services that can lighten your load so you can focus on parenting as much as possible. It's good to give these possible services some thought before you feel completely overwhelmed, stressed by your kids, or are arguing with your ex. Keep in mind that what you might find helpful right now may not be something you need forever. It might be worth the financial outlay for a relatively brief period of time to help make your adjustment to nesting go smoothly.

For example, I suggested that we hire a snow removal service once we divorced, because the kids were young (that is, they couldn't shovel us out themselves, nor could they make themselves breakfast and get ready for school without supervision), we have a long driveway, and their school is notorious for not closing for snow, even when all the other schools around us do. Now that I was single-parenting, I didn't want to be shoveling snow and then getting them ready for school, nor did I want us all to be stuck in the house all day. Before we divorced, Bill did all the shoveling while I focused on the kids. So we hired a snowplow company that promised to have the driveway shoveled by 7 a.m. It was a lifesaver for a couple of bad winters we had those first few years!

However, eventually, the kids got older. *They* could shovel while I (still in my jammies) made breakfast.

A lawn-mowing service was another temporary, but much appreciated, help. When they were younger, neither Bill nor I wanted to leave the kids alone in the house and be out on the mower for two hours. Now they're bigger and one of *them* can be out on the mower.

The first couple of years, Bill hired a nanny—a high school girl we knew—for summer workdays when he had the kids. She drove them around to activities, fed, and entertained them for a few hours every day. They liked her and Bill appreciated the help. I appreciated the time to work on my freelance writing, but I also missed my kids and felt kind of weird about Bill paying someone else to do what I used to always do in the summers. By the third summer, I proposed to Bill—and he agreed—that he "hire" me to do extra parenting hours during the summer (basing my "pay" on the per-night child support rate assigned by the state). I did less freelance work, but still made some money, and—best of all—spent more time with my kids. It was a win for all of us.

Beyond those examples, other types of practical help that you may want to consider or plan for—even if only temporarily—might be:

+ Extra childcare, such as after- or before-school care; a nanny or babysitters; camps for summer or school holidays
+ Food-related help, like grocery delivery or meal kit services
+ Home-related help, like housecleaning, dog walking, or (if you're really lucky) an "Alice" like the one they had on *The Brady Bunch!*

USE THE SUPPORT YOU ALREADY HAVE

I already discussed how to best call on the help of trusted family and friends in chapter 7, "Telling Family and Friends—Step Four." But this is also the moment to use a little bit of resourcefulness and reach out to people who already have your children's best interests in mind and probably know them well.

YOUR CHILDREN'S TEACHERS

Bill and I met with teachers the first year we started nesting, just to let them know what was going on in the kids' home life. We wanted our kids' teachers to know that we were going through a divorce.

We asked their teachers to please keep an extra-close eye on them, especially in terms of changes in emotions or behavior, and to please contact us—both of us—if they had any concerns. We were clear that, even though we were divorcing, we were both still fully on board with parenting our kids together.

A couple of interesting things came out of these conversations. First, the teachers expressed such appreciation for being told about the divorce. They commented that they rarely know what stresses one of their students may be going through outside of school. They feel better prepared to understand and help a child if they have an idea of the bigger picture. Also, I was surprised by how enthusiastic they were about nesting, and that was gratifying. It's often the teachers who are on the front line of children of divorce not having what they need for school because "It's at Mommy's (or Daddy's) house" and being upset or embarrassed—which is emotionally hard on the teachers, too, who are rather helpless in that situation.

It was comforting to me to know that they were keeping a special eye on our kids and knew they could reach out to us as soon as they had any concerns.

PARENTS OF YOUR CHILDREN'S FRIENDS

Of course, there were times that Bill or I needed help with driving the kids somewhere or picking them up, or we needed a place for them to go after school until one of us could get there. The help of other parents was hugely appreciated in those cases. As with the teachers, though, this was about wanting to know that another caring adult was looking out for how my kids were doing even more than needing practical help. I felt that the parents of my kids' best friends had spent a lot of time with my kids (before the divorce) and knew them pretty well. I asked them to please let me know if they noticed anything different in my child's behavior or mood, or if their own child mentioned anything they thought I should know. I also wanted to make sure they understood nesting (most people had never heard of it before us), so they and their children were clear that sometimes Bill was at the house and sometimes I was—and either was fine. They didn't have to keep track of any schedules— just know that our kids were always in the same place and it was always fine to reach out to either Bill or me (or both of us) to schedule playdates, sleepovers, or whatever.

Health and Well-Being Team

Big life changes can throw you off the rails, especially when it comes to staying on track with healthy lifestyle and general well-being. We all know it's important to take care of your own physical and emotional health. Not doing so affects your ability to cope with stress and be the best parent to your children. It may be tricky, though, to maintain it as a priority when you're trying to keep up with your children's schedules and needs, all while working to end your marriage and set up your nesting plan. Plus, you're probably trying to figure out ways to fit other priorities into your week, such as staying on track at work and tending to an aging or ailing parent. And what about doing things that make you happy? Who even has time for that, right?

Medical and mental health professionals are an important part of your team to help you through this challenging stage of life.

EMOTIONAL WELL-BEING: YOU AND YOUR CHILDREN

You may want to let your primary care physician know what you are coping with in your personal life, especially if you feel it is impacting your health or lifestyle choices (more on that below). Your primary care physician can also be an excellent source for referrals to therapists and counselors. That was how I found our marriage counselor when Bill and I first were considering divorce. She has now gone on to be my personal therapist for many years.

Divorce is hard, being—and having—an "ex" is hard, co-parenting is hard. Heck, just being a parent is hard. Then add the unique challenges of nesting (like being around your ex way more than most divorced people are) and it can all get to be too much. Yes, I know it takes time to see a therapist. Early on I had a standing appointment and saw my therapist every two weeks, like clockwork. But over time—a year or so—that began to stretch out to once every three weeks, then gradually to six, then to just whenever I felt I needed to talk something over. But I can't imagine getting this far if I hadn't invested that time early on in having a neutral party help me frame communication with Bill or my kids, prioritize all the issues I was juggling, and help me understand my own emotions. Just having someone to *vent* to for forty-five minutes every once in a while was invaluable!

Therapy helps as you navigate the challenges of divorce, but it can also help you be the best parent possible. "It's beneficial to have support from a neutral party as you work through the dos and don'ts of co-parenting," says family attorney and mediator Brakeman. "Most people think they are a good parent—and most are—but most people haven't been a *divorced* parent before and that's different."

While nesting can greatly alleviate some of the stress that children go through in a traditional divorce, your children may still be dealing with difficult emotions. They may be struggling with the idea of their parents being divorced or be sad that one or the other of you isn't around as much as you used to be.

Even if you don't notice anything medically concerning, it can be a good idea to loop your children's pediatrician into what is going on in their lives. Sometimes stress or anxiety can manifest as health issues, such as digestive problems or bedwetting, and it's best if the medical professional has the full picture to effectively help your child.

Your child's pediatrician is also a good source for recommendations to therapists. Their school's counselor may be a good resource as well. These professionals are all accustomed to working with children in families going through divorce, but the rarity of nesting may mean that you should also explain how you are co-parenting (see chapter 7, "Telling Family and Friends—Step Four").

Perhaps you don't think your children need therapy, and you may be right. Personally, I was motivated to find them a therapist as much to help them as to help *me*. I wanted someone who was a neutral party to give me feedback on how they were processing the divorce and how they *really* felt about our nesting situation.

You know what it's like—this parenting thing. You never know for certain if your kids are doing alright. Most won't confide in their parents about their deepest worries—especially if you're the cause of them—or if they feel they are letting you down or causing you to worry if they tell you how they are actually feeling. This is when a neutral party, who understands kids and their developmental stages can be invaluable.

Soon after we divorced, I was fortunate to find a therapist my two oldest boys connected with. I was referred to her by another mom I knew from school who was a therapist herself. Both my boys liked her right away. They never balked at going to see her. Each only went every six weeks or so, and they always left the appointments in a good mood. And I always left each appointment with a bit of insight into how they were doing (and how I was doing as a parent).

I hadn't gotten around to having the youngest meet with her yet. He was only seven and seemed pretty carefree. I often brought him along to the appointments, but he didn't mind—he liked to play with the toys in the office waiting room.

Eventually, he asked when he could have a turn. I scheduled an appointment, even though he said he didn't have a particular issue in mind to discuss, he "just wanted to see what it's like." ("Hey, the more comfortable they are with therapy now, the better off they'll be in the long run," I told myself. "Someday their future partners will thank me!")

The appointment arrived and I could sense his excitement building as he sat beside me in the waiting room—not playing with the toys at all but staring expectantly down the hallway for her to appear and call us back. Finally, she called his name and he confidently walked down the hall ahead of me. (She'd invited me to sit in on the first part of the session, which he was fine with.)

He strolled into the office and immediately laid himself out prone on her couch, plumped the pillow behind his head, and gazed up at her expectantly.

Where'd he get that idea? I wondered to myself. *Has he been secretly reading old* New Yorker *cartoons?*

She and I shared a glance and stifled smiles. She forged ahead with welcoming him, told him a bit about what therapy means, and asked a few getting-to-know-you questions.

Then she gently broached the topic of the divorce and how we live. He popped up into a seated position and launched into a thorough explanation of nesting.

"That's very interesting," she replied. "What do you think of the way your family lives? It's kind of unusual."

He shrugged indifferently. "I think we seem about the same as any other family."

At the end of his session, she and I spoke alone for a moment. "Each of your kids has the worries typical to others their age: school and friends and fitting in. But I see a lot of children of divorce, and I can tell you, yours are the only ones who have never once brought up the divorce as something that causes stress in their lives."

That was reassuring. Because, even if you feel strongly that nesting is the right thing to do, sometimes it's really great to have it confirmed by someone else.

PHYSICAL WELL-BEING

It's important not to ignore your physical health—even if you feel as if you're constantly short on time. This might mean scheduling your own doctor's appointments on days when you're not on parenting duty. But, at the same time, as you get into the new routine of nesting, don't be too hard on yourself if, at first, you can't keep up your standards of healthy eating and/or exercise.

What you should be on the lookout for is the impulse to "self-medicate" with alcohol or other less-than-healthy behaviors. While it is quite common to turn to whatever helps you relax during stressful times in life (remember my earlier story about my dad commenting on how many beer bottles I was putting in their recycling bin when I lived with them during my separation?), certain choices can also become destructive and severely impact your ability to parent. Relax and safely have fun with friends when you can, of course. But pay attention if your relaxation or stress release is turning into an unhealthy reliance on substances or other destructive behaviors. If you're at all worried about your substance use, it's important to address that immediately by speaking with a professional.

This is also an important time to pay attention to what message your health-related behaviors during a stressful time are sending to your children. Perhaps save the just vegging out in front of the TV—we all need that sometimes!—for when you are out of the nest. When you are on duty at the nest, the attention you pay to your own diet and physical activity sets a good example and sends your children a stronger message than any lecturing you might do. Even better if you can involve them in meal prep, food shopping, physical activities, or time outdoors for some additional one-on-one time with you.

Remember: You are not alone—this team you have compiled is here to help you through the challenges. In relieving your children of much of the burden of a conventional two-home divorce, you are taking on more yourself than ever before. It's okay to ask for help—you deserve it!

IN BRIEF: STEP FIVE

It takes a team to successfully pull off nesting. Find professionals you can trust, who understand your family's goals:

Financial and Legal Help

- Determine which legal or financial team members you may need, based on the plans for your family home and your divorce timeline. Find professionals who listen to you and are supportive of your nesting goals.
- Go in prepared to discuss nesting-specific issues with each of these team members, including your future goals for your children and yourselves, legal and financial responsibility for the maintenance and care of the nest, and how—and when—nesting may end in the future.

Practical Help

- Even with the conveniences provided by nesting, single parenting can be hard. Practical help is invaluable as you begin nesting: Some of this assistance may be only temporary as you transition into nesting (or while your children are young) and might include help with home care or childcare.

- Don't hesitate to call on the help of friends, family, and your children's teachers or other adults in their lives.

Health and Well-Being

- Support in the areas of physical and emotional health for you and your children are critical during this time.
- Therapy helps as you work through the challenges of divorce, and it can also help you be the best parent possible.
- Your children should also have the opportunity to speak with a mental health professional, and you can get a referral from your pediatrician or your school's guidance counselor.
- Pay attention to any emerging health concerns in your children, as physical symptoms may be a sign of stress.
- Don't let your own health fall completely by the wayside, but at the same time, don't be too hard on yourself if at first you can't keep up your standards of healthy eating and/or exercise.
- Speak with a professional immediately if you find yourself drinking alcohol excessively and more frequently than before, or if you're engaging in other potentially destructive behaviors.

CHAPTER 9

The Trial Period—Step Six

You can plan all you want—and planning *is* important—but you won't really know how nesting works for you and your family until you start doing it. The trial period allows you time before you are fully committed to nesting to identify the things that aren't working well and to attempt to find ways to make them work better. Challenges can arise from logistics (like moving yourself back and forth between two places), emotions (like grieving for your old life), and others that are discussed farther on in this chapter. There can also be surprisingly difficult challenges that come up from seemingly innocuous things, as Bill and I found when we began nesting.

I asked Bill what he remembered most from our trial period. "The stress of laundry! I had never done it before," he says emphatically. Just to clarify, he *had* done laundry before, way back when he was a single guy. The difference was now he was doing laundry for himself and a household with three boys. I had been accustomed to it because laundry had always been one of my chores during our married life. But it was all new to Bill. "There was just so *much* of it. On top of all the other stuff I was dealing with—the divorce, the extra parenting, kids' homework, working full time—it was super stressful to have to always be doing the damn laundry, too."

The boys' school uniforms added to the hassle. Their school requires all kids to wear white shirts on Wednesdays (they can wear other colors on other days). The number of Wednesdays in those early days when Bill or one of the kids was digging a dirty white shirt out of the hamper and wiping it off to wear again were countless, and stressful. Also, because the school clothes all looked the same, Bill could never keep track of which clothes went to which boy's room. Laundry was a surprisingly big ordeal—especially if, like Bill, you weren't used to doing it all the time, as I had been.

His laundry situation was really stressing *me* out, too. Because either an Everest-size pile was waiting for me when I got to the house or because Bill would call me to complain about how much laundry there was to do. Sometimes one of the boys would text me at 7 a.m.: I DON'T HAVE ANY SCHOOL SHIRTS! I was at my apartment—what was I supposed to do about that?!

So after a couple of months of this, we came up with a system to help him. Instead of letting it pile up in each boy's room until Bill had time to do it, laundry was collected every day—by our middle son (the other two were given an additional daily chore to keep things fair). I bought a four-section laundry hamper, and each kid knew which bin to put their dirty clothes in. Bill's assignment to keep him from getting overwhelmed: Do one load per day (whichever bin was the fullest). Put it in the washing machine before breakfast, put the load in the dryer sometime during the day, fold at night after dinner. Also, I started marking the labels of all their clothes with a Sharpie—one dot for the oldest, two for the middle, three for the youngest. (I cannot take credit for that idea—I read it in an old *Family Circle* magazine at the pediatrician's office.)

At first in the trial period, you will probably be overwhelmed because now nesting is no longer a theoretical concept. You are *in* it! That means that if something unexpectedly becomes challenging, you will need to come up with a solution. Depending on the severity of the challenge, it may be something you need to address right away (for example, if one of the children is really struggling with the change) or it may be something you can take a bit of time to figure out how to adapt (like doing laundry or getting dinner on the table at the same time every evening). In either case, it's best if you both can talk about the problem and devise a solution together. Setting a schedule to regularly review how things are going—at least at first, weekly is probably a good idea—can encourage you to identify your biggest challenges and know there will be an opportunity to assess them and revise as needed.

As for the length of your trial period: I think generally at least three months would be a useful gauge for most families. Nester Kate says, "We piloted nesting over the summer. My older daughter and I went on a road trip for part of the time, my ex stayed with the younger." Kate and her ex had already been co-parenting in two separate homes for a couple of years, so each was used to doing the school and evening routines on their own. If one of you hasn't had as much experience handling school-day routines on your own, I would suggest scheduling the trial run over both an in-school time and a break time. This will help both of you determine how to juggle the demands of your careers and schedule along with school-day routines and the days when the kids are not in school. You need a well-oiled machine to cope with the morning rush to get everyone out the door on time and you need a plan for more relaxed mornings when your kids are hanging around the home.

Of course, the longer you can do trial nesting, the longer you will have to adapt and to adjust. As mentioned earlier, Bill and I had set our trial period at one year because that was the length of time for which we'd leased the non-nest apartment. We were meeting regularly to assess how things were going for us and how we thought the kids were doing. I do think having the whole year (it ran from February to February) helped us hit our stride as we worked through all the usual family scheduling things—holidays, kids' birthdays, work travel, illnesses, snow days, school breaks—but as a nesting family.

Easing into the Transition Period

The ages of your children often determine how easily they'll be able to transition into nesting and what issues may arise once the trial period begins. We looked at this in some detail in chapter 5, "Talking to Your Children About Your Divorce and Nesting— Step Two."

Nester Kate's fourteen-year-old daughter was concerned about what others would think about her family living in this unusual way. "She thought her friends would think it was weird," says Kate. "But, no, all her friends think it's cool and the ones with divorced parents are jealous."

My children were younger than Kate's when we began nesting. They were less concerned about explaining divorce and nesting to friends and more concerned about how their daily routines would be affected. I felt they needed extra reassurance that they would see each of us regularly. Bill and I planned out in advance how we would ease them into the new nesting schedule—me in the house Wednesday morning through Saturday afternoon; then Dad Saturday afternoon to Wednesday morning.

As noted in chapter 5, we—together—told our kids about our divorce and nesting and then had a family dinner together. I didn't want them to feel "We told you we're divorcing and now Mom's outta here!" so I spent the night at the house that night and stuck around Saturday morning to make them breakfast. Then we began our nesting schedule, just as we had described it to them. I left the house that afternoon (the apartment wasn't ready yet, so I was still staying at my parents'). Sunday they were with their dad all day and he got them off to school Monday morning. I picked them up from school the first couple of days. Even though those were Bill's days, we wanted to reassure them as to how close I was and how frequently they would continue to see me. I was back in the house Wednesday morning to get them ready for school, just as we told them I would be.

That Saturday, I got to stay at the apartment for the first time. The boys and Bill helped move some things in. They even brought the dog along to check it out. I wanted them to see what a short drive away it was from the house and to have an image in their heads of where Dad or I were when we weren't with them.

This transition time into nesting can be challenging for you, perhaps even more than it is for your kids. Navigating single-parenting for the first time—even if it is only for a few nights in a row—can be very different from having another parent around.

HERE ARE A FEW GENERAL PARENTING REMINDERS TO KEEP IN MIND AS NESTING BEGINS:

+ Try not to automatically delegate parenting
  responsibilities to your oldest/most competent child. Of

course, kids need to have a sense of responsibility in the family—but it's not their job to take over parenting tasks. For example, it may be tempting to have the older child monitor the younger kids doing their homework. But is managing their younger siblings a fair responsibility when they have their own homework to do? Is it something you would have considered a parental responsibility when you were still married? Find other ways they can contribute to home and family life—taking the dog out or emptying the dishwasher, for example—and have chores spread evenly across each of your children (age-appropriately, of course), so that one doesn't feel that the other kids are getting off easy.

+ Be aware that you may need to spend more time with your children than you did before the divorce, and you may have to be more patient and understanding with them. Even though you are nesting and trying to keep their lives consistent, the idea of divorce—or just missing the other parent—may still trouble them, upset sleep schedules, or cause problems at school.

+ That said, continue to provide your kids with rules, limits, and reasonable consequences for misbehavior as you did before.

Common Pitfalls

As with parenting or life in general, there will always be challenges—ones that you just deal with for a period of time because you have to, or because you haven't figured out (yet) how to improve the situation. Almost all nesters face these common challenges—they're par for the course. Some are logistical, some are emotional (some are a combination of both). But, as we've considered so many times before, are they worth being a challenge for *you*, so your kids have fewer stresses in their lives?

LOGISTICAL CHALLENGES

Ah, "transition day." The day you (and your stuff) either move into the nest, or into your out-of-the-nest space. No matter how much of a minimalist nesting has inspired you to become, you will need to devote some time to packing and then unpacking your belongings and settling into the new space. As your kids would have had to do if they were moving back and forth between two houses.

Since Kate and her ex did the traditional two-house approach for several years before they began nesting, she has a particular appreciation for what it entails. "On transition day, I like bearing the burden on behalf of the kids instead of them doing it," she says. "I remember what it was like for them to have to pack and transition in and out of two houses. They remember, as well, and they have said they appreciate the effort I make so they don't have to."

I once heard someone on a podcast who was recently divorced describe how her four-year-old daughter's life changed and how her daughter would need to get accustomed to living in two different homes. It's "like she's a nonstop business traveler, but not racking up any frequent-flier miles," the mom said of her child. "And she'll be doing it every week for the next fourteen years."

I never had a job that required frequent travel, but Bill did for many years, so I saw firsthand how the frequent traveler has to have a set routine (and a supply of duplicates of toiletries, etc.) to make that regular "in and out of a suitcase" lifestyle work. To avoid any additional stress from this way of life he had to stick to a set packing routine. That mindset is what I applied to my own transition days. I've been doing it so many years it's almost (but not always!) second nature.

As I've mentioned, I'm "based" out of my apartment; that is, all my stuff is there. At the house, the guest bathroom and bedroom in the basement are mine. I've (minimally) decorated those rooms so they feel like my personal space. The only clothes that "live" there all the time are some old work clothes in the back of my closet for yard work or house projects (I never have to do that at my apartment!). In the bathroom, I have whatever was cheap to duplicate (toothpaste, mouthwash, cotton balls) or too bulky (hair dryer) to lug back and forth. I guess I could duplicate more, but I never get around to it.

For transition days I have a basic three-, sometimes four-, bag system: Bag #1: Toiletries, Bag #2: Clothes and shoes, Bag #3: Work stuff.

> **Bag #1: Toiletries.** Contact solution, makeup, hair products, and the twenty-seven (approximately) vials and tubes of anti-aging products I must use on my face (thanks for those worry wrinkles, married life).
>
> **Bag #2: Clothes and shoes.** This got a lot easier when Covid hit and I stopped doing anything that required real clothes. I basically just went from wearing jammies at night to leggings and T-shirts during the day. However, in times before, when I needed to have clothes I could wear to go talk to grown-ups, I would check the weather forecast and pick something fancier—like jeans and a black sweater and real shoes (not Uggs or flip-flops). You see? I have embraced minimalism!
>
> **Bag #3: Work stuff.** Laptop, keyboard and laptop stand (to avoid neck pain and carpal tunnel syndrome), chargers and headphones, various folders for work projects, house/personal financial paperwork, Kindle or actual book, and journal.
>
> *Sometimes* **Bag #4.** Dirty laundry and/or winter gear bag. There have been occasions when I haven't had time to do

laundry before I change locations, or sometimes it's winter here and I have to haul an extra coat or boots.

As mentioned, this packing routine is almost—but not always—second nature. Many times I'd arrive at one place, only to find that I'd left a charger or a pair of shoes at the other place. One time, I got to the house, dumped my bags down in the hall, and realized I'd forgotten my laptop back at my apartment! (This sticks in my mind because my laptop is like an appendage that I can't live without—it's always with me.)

Bill was in the laundry room and heard my expletive as I came in, even though our eldest was loudly practicing his bass guitar in the living room. Bill asked what was wrong and I called into the laundry room (over the sound of the Red Hot Chili Peppers or some such) that I'd forgotten my laptop and would have to drive back to my apartment.

"Well, at least you're not keeping track of three kids' stuff," he called out into the hall.

"Right!" I yelled back.

The bass playing abruptly stopped—though the song was still blaring from the stereo—and our eldest son Jack hollered from the living room, "What was that about 'kids' stuff'?"

("How do kids always hear when you're talking about *them*?" I marveled.)

I yelled back, "Dad and I were just saying how nice it is that we only have to move our stuff in and out of the house, instead of you three kids moving all your stuff!"

"Yeah, that would suck," was the sotto voce reply.

The bass started up again. Bill and I just shook our heads at each other as I grabbed my keys to drive back to my apartment.

TRANSITION DAY ROUTINES AND RITUALS

Nesting parents, particularly when the in-and-out routine is new, often say they don't like going into the other, non-nest living space—it makes them feel lonely or depressed or just "not at home." Nor do they feel exactly at home in the nest any longer. I remember Bill saying that he had vaguely depressed/lonely feelings whenever he went to the apartment we were sharing. Personally, I loved going there (I still do). It was nice to get some peace and quiet. Then, after a couple of days to regroup, I missed the kids and was ready to be back in the mix of it all.

At the house, which felt sort of weird to both of us, we discussed removing reminders of our marriage. But ultimately that was more work that it was worth—after eighteen years of marriage you have memories on practically everything! But in an effort to alleviate emotional reactions we became more mindful of putting our personal stuff in our own rooms before the other person returned to the nest.

For me—and other nesters have made similar comments—having a consistent system of actions to transition in and out at each place helps me feel more settled. There's a sense of ritualistically—not to sound too new agey, woo-woo here—establishing the space as *yours*, even though it's temporary, that is comforting. I recommend creating some rituals or set transitional activities to help ease some of the "weirdness" and help you enjoy the time at each place more.

When transitioning into the house, once I've said hello to the kids and the dog and touched base with Bill on what needs addressing, I always set up my little workspace on "Mom's counter" in the kitchen next to the kitchen table where I do all my writing. It's just a space to charge my laptop and my phone and arrange whatever research or reading materials I need, but I just don't feel officially "in" until I have it set up. Because I come in and out of the house frequently these days, if my work stuff is set up, that means I'm really "on duty." (I also have to reload the dishwasher the way I like it. Since I'll be the next one to unload it, I want it done right!)

Transitioning back into my apartment, I follow a similar routine. Though the whole place is just my stuff, something about setting up my work desk again tells me I'm "home." I often take the time when I get there to enjoy the quiet and lack of distractions—I light a favorite candle and do some journaling to process whatever I had to set aside in my mind while I was focused on being Mom.

Nester Michael describes how he is trying to make the nest and his space outside of the nest both feel more like his own space. He says, "For the condo, I'm a book lover so one of the first things I did was buy a bookshelf and bring over all my books to surround myself with. I describe it as the literary version of comfort food! My ex always preferred quiet time in the evening, so when I'm here I blast my favorite music like I always wanted to. At home [the nest], I'm becoming more comfortable doing things just for me, even though it's primarily a space for the kids. We have a great backyard (something I don't have at my condo) so I've been grilling a lot and occasionally sit outside with a drink after the kids go to bed. And I recently hosted a get-together for my work colleagues. I've always been super social, and I saw it as something to do for *me* in a space that I still love and feel connected to. I'm trying to identify the parts of our home that I can reclaim when I'm there and make them feel more like my own."

DIFFERENT STANDARDS AND PRIORITIES AT THE NEST

As anyone who's ever lived with someone else knows, people have different standards about how they live: cleanliness, organization, what they eat. Since you lived with your co-parent for some length of time before nesting, you likely have a pretty good idea of what their standards are. All the ground rules you may write up beforehand aren't going to completely change this aspect of your ex's personality.

It may be frustrating, but unless the kids are in danger or unhappy in their home because of one parent's poor housekeeping or penchant for fast food, this may be an issue that you'll have to agree to disagree on. Or come up with some solutions together, especially if the differences are causing you a lot of stress or making it difficult for you to focus on your parenting time. You may find outsourcing some help to alleviate your stress is worth it—and you shouldn't feel guilty about it! We look at some ideas for possible "practical help" in chapter 9, "The Trial Period—Step Six." You also could get a bit creative and adjust responsibilities or financial arrangements between the two of you—sort of a "bartering" over which tasks stress you out and which ones you don't mind doing (or which you are willing to pay someone else to do).

SOME EXAMPLES FROM NESTING FAMILIES:

+ One parent pays for a cleaning service at the end of their week in the house, because they don't like cleaning and would rather focus on the kids.
+ One parent does all the laundry and straightening up but hates to cook; the other parent makes extra meals for them to pull from the fridge or freezer.

At our house, Bill really hates when the hallway has dog hair in it (for some reason, I don't notice it as much as he does). He used to complain every time he came in the house that he *had* to vacuum right away. Bill recently decided it was worth it to "hire" the youngest to vacuum the hall every other day, whether he is in the house or not. Fine by me.

Even if there are disparities between how the two of you keep house, the consistency for the kids makes it easier for them to handle some differences between each parent's time there. It was my experience that, while what condition the kitchen was in when I came in may have been important to me, the kids certainly weren't affected by differences in housekeeping or differences in how Dad did some things as opposed to Mom. As long as *their* important things were covered—getting to school on time and having the right stuff with them, seeing their friends whenever they could, and hanging out and relaxing at the house with the dog every day—they were fine.

SCHEDULES

The aspect of scheduling that seems to cause the most frustration and conflict for nesting parents is what happens on transition days. Is the other parent there when they said they would be? Is the on-duty parent ready to clear our when the incoming parent shows up?

Tedd recalls that this was an issue from their early years of nesting: "Jean is a night person and I'm a morning person. It would make me mad that she was never ready to leave when I would show up on the switchover Sundays at noon."

Jean agrees: "I'm terrible with time management. The internal pressure of always wanting to have the house ready was very stressful."

"After a while of this, it occurred to one of us—I don't remember who—that we should make Monday after I got off work the switchover time. That gave Jean all day to get ready to leave," says Tedd.

This has been an ongoing issue for Bill and me over the years, mainly because he traveled a lot for work before the pandemic, so there were canceled and delayed flights all the time. It was annoying for me, but not anything I could control.

It's still an issue we struggle with sometimes. Correction: *I* struggle with it—he's fine! He's more loosey-goosey about time than I am. If I say, "I'll be there at 4," I'm there at 4. "Midafternoon" is about as specific as Bill likes to get. But I'm always driving over from my apartment which is ten easy minutes away. He's coming back from his girlfriend's in another city. There may be rain, or construction, or an accident to throw everything off.

The thing is, I really like nesting. I really like Bill's girlfriend. I think he's great with the kids. So, it took some nagging, but I've finally gotten him to at least text me when he's on his way to let me know if there's a particular holdup. I try not to get too annoyed if the complication was that he *had* to stop for soft-serve ice cream at that middle-of-nowhere stand that is "world famous."

EMOTIONAL CHALLENGES

Nesting can stir up some emotional issues for you or your ex, which may be stronger than in the traditional two-house approach. As in so many things, having to deal with these emotions yourself, rather than putting more emotional burdens on your children, is the trade-off. At some point, you are likely to experience frustration with the lack of boundaries and how involved you still are in each other's lives, sadness when you come across reminders of the life you used to have, anxiety (or anger) over other people being in the nest and/or your ex starting to date.

PRIVACY AND BOUNDARIES

We discussed the issues of privacy and boundaries in chapter 6, "Establishing Ground Rules—Step Three," and in chapter 8's legal team section. Ideally, you can trust that your ex won't be going through your things when you're not at the nest (and vice versa). If privacy is an ongoing problem in your trial period, it could be reasonable grounds for ending nesting and certainly should be discussed, perhaps with the help of a therapist.

What may come out more during the trial period are the more innocuous breaches of privacy or boundaries. Even something like knowing that your unopened mail or your grocery purchases are seen by the other person may feel weird as you are working on separating your lives from each other.

Being divorced or separated takes some getting used to; it may be difficult to know what's still okay to ask about and what is not. For example, asking "What'd you do last night?" may feel fraught with layers of meaning. Try to be cognizant of why you are *really* asking a question, and maybe just keep it to yourself. Don't comment on mail you've seen ("*Another* box came from Zappos!") or things you've heard ("The neighbor said he saw you at Ruth's Chris steakhouse last night. Fancy"). Unless it's house- or kid-related, try to interact in a neutral fashion, as if you just worked in the same office or something like that, especially in the early stages, after the end of your marriage when emotions are raw (Ha! Steakhouse pun). Eventually, you won't really care where your ex eats dinner or how many shoes they order.

On the flip side, if your ex asks you questions you're not comfortable with, it's okay not to answer—unless it is related to the children or the nest. It's even better if you can kindly and maturely point out to them that it's not an appropriate question.

GRIEF FOR YOUR OLD LIFE

A lot is different now. Maybe you are missing the feeling of being married. Maybe you are missing being with your ex. Maybe you are fine with being divorced but miss spending time with your mutual friends or your ex's family (I'm raising my hand for that one). Maybe you miss being in your home all the time. These feelings of loss you may only get over in time, and with the help of therapy. Eventually, new and happy things will fill your "off-duty" time and it will get easier.

Also, almost certainly, you are missing being around your kids as much as you used to—that's a tougher one.

"Starting off was hard for me," says Michael. "As a teacher, I had a lot of time with my kids before the divorce. Fifty/fifty custody was really hard for me to adjust to."

Missing the kids can be ameliorated in many ways: calls and Facetiming, stopping by the nest to see them (if your ex is okay with that), volunteering at school (I did this a lot when we first divorced—sometimes I was at the school every day and would see at least one, if not all three, of the boys).

Something that helps me, when I'm feeling blue about not being with them, is knowing that I'm a much more present parent since we started nesting. I've had a little bit of me time when I'm out of the nest, so I fully give myself to being with them when I'm at the house, with no resentment. And, I'm not trying to be a wife at the same time—which can be distracting, or at least it was for me. I'm just Mom and I love that.

DATING

Many nesters designate the trial period as a time when no "new adults" (or however you want to phrase it) are introduced to the children. In chapter 10, "Down the Road: Challenges, Milestones, and Transitioning out of Nesting," we'll look at recommendations for ways to best introduce a new partner to your children. Most nesting arrangements allow plenty of non-nest time, when either parent can pursue dating. You don't have to deprive yourself, just be respectful of the nest and of your ex's feelings.

It's not easy knowing that your ex is dating—especially if you aren't. You may not feel emotionally ready to date and it's hurtful to know that they had no such compunction. Once again, I'm giving my go-to advice (sorry if it's getting tiresome), but these feelings about the other person dating are just going to take some time to get over, and therapy is a big help. Give yourself time. Parenting your children well during this transitional time is the most important—and rewarding—thing you can do.

Suzanne recalls an unexpected reaction to her ex's dating. She was out of town with their kids and told him it would be fine if his new girlfriend stayed at the house while they were gone. "I was pleased with myself for being so open-minded and generous. I didn't begrudge him a new relationship," she says. But when she got back home, there was a pink razor in the shower that wasn't hers.

"At first, I thought it was kind of funny—would be a good story to tell friends over drinks. But some of them said, 'She's sending you a message, marking her territory.' I'd soon whipped myself into a frenzy, even though it had been *my* idea for her to stay there!"

Suzanne was surprised by the anger and suspicion she felt, but she recognized that it was a reaction stirred up by others and took the time to let herself process it, rather than pick a fight with her ex or his girlfriend. "Now that I know her, I'm sure it wasn't some hidden message, just forgetfulness," says Suzanne.

Suzanne makes an excellent point as well: that sometimes other people—like well-meaning friends looking for an entertaining conversation over drinks—can arouse your emotions because of *their* opinions about a situation.

Trial Period Assessment and Reassessing

Ideally, you have been communicating during this trial period about things that need to be addressed immediately, like the children's schedules or household-related topics. It's also a good idea to set a scheduled "touching base" meeting to make time to really sort out, outside of the rush of day-to-day life, how things are going for all of you. Though Bill and I had set our nesting trial period for one year, we scheduled our first "official" assessment meeting at the one-month mark. A month felt like long enough for us to get a feel for the routine but still identify a number of issues to discuss. You may want to meet sooner, if there have been a lot of unexpected stresses—or if the two of you don't communicate regularly. If possible, keep this meeting focused on the nesting situation, rather than getting into emotional topics. To keep on topic and avoid contention, it may be best to meet at a neutral spot, like a coffee shop; or if you do meet at the nest, do it at a time when the children are not there.

THE FIRST MEETING AGENDA SHOULD ADDRESS:

How are the kids doing?

Since the main point of nesting is to be focused on the children, this is the #1 question. Check in on the basics of how they are doing: sleeping, eating, keeping up with schoolwork, getting along socially, cooperating with siblings. Also, share any questions or worries they've brought up that you may want to address together. While I think it's best if children are not at this meeting, it can be helpful before you meet to ask them how they think things are going (agree with your spouse ahead of time who will talk with the kids about this). As discussed before, older children may be more likely to share their concerns or give some suggestions. For younger children, you may need to gauge how well they are adjusting based on their behavior—for example, changes in sleep issues or new, unreasonable fears that have developed—rather than on what they actually say to you.

Any ground rules to loosen up?

Perhaps certain cleaning standards or household chores should be less important than you originally thought, or maybe they're less of a priority as the kids adjust to this new schedule. I recall that we quickly gave up on the "your groceries/my groceries" approach (separate shelves in the pantry, the refrigerator, etc.); with everything else we were adjusting to, it just wasn't worth the effort of keeping track of who opened what or telling the kids they couldn't have something they could see in the pantry.

Any particularly frustrating or challenging issues?

Maybe some things that have come up have caused unexpected stress (like laundry!) or, in hindsight, weren't handled very well. I mentioned in chapter 6 that how Bill and I communicated (he called or texted whenever he felt stressed, and I jumped to always answer him immediately) caused me a lot of stress and him a lot of anxiety. As I noted, we eventually worked out a better system. Looking back, we let this go on way too long—perhaps understandably, because it was the communication pattern that had been established during our marriage. As we began nesting, it exacerbated our stress for quite a while and made communicating much more challenging and frustrating than it should have been. With the help of my therapist, and some honest conversations with Bill, we established better ways of communicating.

If you're encountering unexpected challenges, bring some ideas for how to handle these in the future. Or if it's a very complicated issue, agree to both think about what to do about the issue and discuss it again at another time. Resolving larger issues may take several conversations.

Nester Suzanne suggests, "As you're figuring out your nesting situation, get as clear as possible about what your differences are, what your problems are. Then work to set it up to solve those biggest challenges, to minimize them, not make them worse."

Review what is working well and congratulate yourselves for your hard work.

It's always good to end on a positive note and recognize what is working well. It may be the things you expected, such as that nesting seems to be helping the kids adjust to the divorce, or that it's nice you aren't spending as much money as if you'd set up two separate households by now. It may be things that are a bit unexpected. I recall Bill mentioning that he liked that our new situation had "forced" him to become more engaged in the boys' schoolwork (an area that had defaulted to me in the past). He liked talking with the kids more specifically about what they were doing; and he appreciated being more involved in communicating with their teachers and getting to know them better. I found that I really enjoyed dinnertime with just the three kids. There was just a different flow to our conversations than when Dad was there. Also, do make a point to recognize the efforts that each of you have put toward trying to make nesting work. A little appreciation goes a long way in this process of working together.

WATCH OUT FOR RED FLAGS

You may have seen (and possibly ignored) some "red flags" early on in your planning, indicating that nesting may be too challenging for you and your ex. These may be ongoing issues related to the challenges in your marriage or issues that cropped up as you began the divorce process. Perhaps you hoped they would go away once the divorce was behind you. Perhaps you hoped your ex would be inspired to step up and behave better now that they had responsibility for the kids. Those are not unreasonable hopes. But the well-being of the children is the ultimate goal. If they do not seem to be doing well, is it related to one or the other parent's issues about the divorce? Is that parent willing to work on those issues?

"The reasons that led up to the divorce are worth considering. Will sharing the house continue the conflict?" asks attorney and mediator Christopher Forrest. "If one parent is hurt so badly that they are having trouble getting over it, it makes it difficult to cooperate and collaborate on parenting. Not impossible, but it may take a lot of work on the part of both parents."

If you are not seeing improvements, or your ex is not willing to work on making changes during the trial period, these are warning signs of larger co-parenting and communication issues that need to be addressed sooner rather than later, and preferably with the oversight of a therapist or family counselor. Some of these red flags include:

+ Either parent refusing to stick to ground rules, with no reason or alternative suggestion
+ Either parent breaking promises or being dishonest
+ Either parent speaking badly about the other to the children
+ The children showing marked changes in behavior or strong reluctance to be with one parent or the other—of course, if a child reports abuse or neglect, you should stop nesting immediately and notify your legal professional.

Perhaps nesting is not feasible for you at this time. Perhaps you are not in an emotional place to "essentially put the kids first, over everything," as nester Lauren describes it.

In most cases, the key aspects to ending it are:

+ Agreeing together to end it
+ Making a plan for when it will end and what the new co-parenting arrangement will be
+ Communicating that plan together to the children with specifics about how and when they will be affected.;

However, with luck and the good groundwork you've laid already, I am hopeful you will be moving forward with nesting. You may find, as we did, that the trial period presents some unexpected experiences that turn into new traditions and lifelong happy memories for all of you.

Like our first nesting Christmas, eight months into our trial period.

Our divorce settlement had the boilerplate "each parent taking turns having the kids on alternate holidays, alternate years" language. Frankly, with all the divorce, nesting, and work stuff of that first year, I hadn't given the upcoming holiday season much thought. But as it got closer, Bill said he'd been thinking that having the kids to himself alternate years was not nearly as important as keeping Christmas traditions alive and well for them. Our boys were still young enough to be *really* into Christmas. Since we were nesting, it was the path of least resistance (that's a theme with me, isn't it?) to just do something along the lines of what we'd always done. We asked the kids which traditions were most important to them, which things they wanted us to definitely do together as a family. Of course, they expected Christmas morning presents, they didn't care so much about setting up the tree or wrapping presents, but we were a bit surprised at how adamant they were about the "Italian Feast" (as we call it) staying the same.

A word on this Feast. It's not only delicious, but also honors the boys' Italian heritage through Bill's family. Though I'm the one who does most of the cooking even though I don't have a drop of Italian blood. But I love doing it. Bill's mom is, sadly, no longer with us, but I was fortunate to learn a lot of classic recipes from her: homemade "gravy" (tomato sauce) with meatballs and braciola (stuffed, rolled flank steak), eggplant parmesan, lasagna, stuffed calamari, and handmade manicotti.

The Feast starts off right after presents are opened Christmas morning, with me at the stove cooking "Grandma's Christmas Eve Shrimp." That's what this dish is always called, no matter what day of the year it's made. The shrimp never actually make it to the table, as the boys learned from their dad to hover around the stove and eat them as soon as they come out of the frying pan—saying "ow! ow! ow!" and "hot! hot! hot!" with every purloined shrimp. I just shake my head and add more to the pan, just like Fran did all those years when she was equally as exasperated by Bill as I am with my own sons (and their dad).

The other recipes take a lot of prep work. I start making batches of "gravy" for the freezer weeks in advance. Bill and I tag-team making all the other dishes in the few days leading up to Christmas.

So, of course, for them, we did it all again that year. As I was prep-cooking in advance, I remember thinking, *Well, this will be nice for them, for continuity. And it gives Bill and me another year to figure out how to do the alternating-holidays thing.*

But as we were cleaning up together *after* the Feast, laughing with the kids in the crowded, messy kitchen—of course the big, creepy fish platter had made an appearance once again; of course Dad was teased yet again for the time he left the braciola on the counter to cool and the dog ate it while he went to have a nap—I said, "This has been pretty frickin' awesome, right? Should we do it again next year?"

"Of course!"

And here we are many years later—eight as I write this—and we're already discussing if we're doing eggplant parmesan or lasagna for this year's Feast. "Or both!" as the boys say.

Things are changing. The kids are older and actually help with the cooking and the cleanup, and we go through more wine than we used to. The dog that ate the braciola many years ago died last year (from old age, not from eating braciola!) and we have a new dog who, so far, has better manners—but we'll see if that holds true when we get to the pre-Feast cooking days.

More changes are on the way, no doubt, as our kids move more and more into their own lives. But I never would have guessed—and am so grateful—that when we decided to all be together for that first nesting Christmas, we would have had all these precious years since of enjoying it together again and again.

IN BRIEF: STEP SIX

The trial period is the time to work out the kinks of your nesting plan, identify any big challenges that need to be addressed, and, especially, the time to be proud of all you have accomplished for your children and the future of your family.

A jointly-agreed-to trial period will help you determine whether nesting is the right decision for your family. Choose a period of time that will give you and your ex a good sense of how schedules and routines will work.

+ At least three months and up to a year to settle into a routine
+ The time frame should include both school time and school breaks

To help your kids transition into nesting, have frequent and regular conversations with your ex on the most important topics:

+ Your kids' schedules, activities, and upcoming important homework or tests (if your kids need monitoring in that area)
+ Any concerns about how the kids are adapting, or if either of you have noticed changes in behavior

(sleeping, eating) or problems with siblings, friends, or at school
✦ If nesting rules are still working and if any of the rules need to be changed
✦ Whether there is need to find paid extra help, temporarily, if certain household tasks are too time-consuming or stressful

Remember: The trial period will include challenges that are both logistical and emotional in nature, so maintain open communication, and remain patient and respectful with your ex. Also, come up with ways to make transition day a predictable routine to minimize these challenges and stay positive about the arrangement. Always celebrate your successes.

CHAPTER 10

Down the Road: Challenges, Milestones, and Transitioning Out of Nesting—Step Seven

I f your nesting trial period has been successful—and I hope it has!—it's time to think ahead to the future. Perhaps you and your ex have agreed to an end date for nesting. Alternatively, perhaps you've agreed that nesting is working well for your family for now, and you don't have a specific idea for how long you'll stick with it. That seems to be where most nesting families are—doing it for as long as it makes sense for the needs of the children.

In either case, even though you have hit your stride with the ins and outs of nesting, there will be challenges ahead—because those are just part of life. In some cases, nesting may complicate these issues; in others, nesting may help you and your kids more easily weather the storm. The same factors that led to a successful launch of nesting—prioritizing the needs of your children and being open to creative solutions—will continue to serve you well as you move into the next stage and toward, eventually, ending the nesting. Even though you and your ex will increasingly each be pursuing your non-coupled lives, open communication and collaboration will continue to be the foundation of successful co-parenting.

Common Changes and Challenges

You just don't know, obviously, what the future will throw your way. Career paths don't always continue as expected, either by choice or by circumstance. Finances can be affected by changes to careers or by other unforeseen life challenges. There may be emotional or medical challenges that can change your family.

In this chapter we'll consider some of these factors that arise during longer-term nesting—as well as the many benefits of sticking with it. We'll also look at when nesting could or should end and how best to approach that. As always, prioritizing your children, thinking creatively, and communicating openly will help you best navigate your nesting future.

CAREERS AND FINANCIAL ISSUES

Your trial period helped you sort out the specifics and address problems of the financial aspects of nesting successfully at that point in the life of your family. As time goes by, there will almost certainly be reasons to revisit the arrangement you first set up. Changes may be needed because of choices you or your co-parent makes; for example, finding a new and better job, deciding to go back to work after being a stay-at-home parent, or pursuing additional schooling to further your career or embark on a new career. Ideally, any changes to the nesting situation that are driven by choices have been discussed and planned for with the other parent well in advance. Career changes may also be unexpected, like being laid off, your company moving to another state, the economy affecting your business's revenues, or you or your ex-spouse becoming injured or sick and unable to work. Any of these can impact your financial situation, your schedule or living arrangements, or other aspects of your nesting arrangement.

Finances may also change unexpectedly, from things like a totaled car, an emergency repair to the home, you or your child requiring long-term medical care, or the need to care for aging parents. Financial priorities may shift as children get older and need their own cars, go to college or explore career opportunities, and get married or start their own families (I know that sounds crazy, but if you have widely spaced children age-wise, as we do, it's completely possible that the oldest could be getting married while you are still nesting with the youngest).

You may have planned for some of this (such as how you will pay for the kids' college educations) in your divorce settlement, but you almost certainly will have some surprises ahead as well. You may be able to work out finances, living arrangements, or schedule adjustments between the two of you. If it is a challenge for you to work this out together, it may be worth the cost to revisit your agreement with your mediator or attorney.

An example from our experience: about five years into our nesting, Bill changed jobs. He told me in advance that he was considering a change and kept me apprised of how the interview process was going. We talked about the aspects of the job that could affect the kids and our nesting arrangement, such as the potential for more and longer work-related travel, and discussed ways in which we thought we could make that work. When he learned about how different the new compensation package would be from his previous job, however, we decided it was worth the time and cost to have our attorneys review the child support agreement in light of these changes. At that time, we also had the attorneys spell out a plan for college tuition and car needs—which we had not addressed in our first settlement agreement. Generally, Bill and I pride ourselves on being able to solve complex problems together, but with the hot-button issue of money and the complications of how differently he was going to be compensated, it was definitely worth the cost and effort to have legal professionals sort that out for us.

ONGOING CHALLENGES

Ideally nesting is making your co-parenting life simpler in many ways. Sometimes, however, the nesting situation raises issues that you thought were behind you or come as a surprise.

The problems you had as a couple don't magically go away, even after years of nesting (this was touched on in chapter 4, "Agreeing to Nest with Your Spouse/Soon-to-Be-Ex—Step One"). These may involve ongoing, complicated emotional issues (more on this below), or more mundane things, like differences in commitments to housekeeping that will never be resolved. When I asked Kate what about nesting has been the hardest thing for her to deal with, she notes, "Nothing related to the emotions of cohabitation with my ex, actually. But when things start to slack in the housekeeping, which isn't that often, but when it does, I resent having those feelings from our married years—I don't want to feel like I am still taking care of a slob."

If things like housekeeping and household chore responsibilities are adding more anxiety to your life as nesting goes on, you may need to address them in new and different ways, as we discussed in chapter 9, "The Trial Period—Step Six." For example, if you know your co-parent is dealing with extra stress in their life temporarily, you may want to just loosen your standards. If it's more of an ongoing issue, you may need to revisit your ground rules, *together*, to reassess what's realistic for each of you to do, what the kids could begin to do more of, or what may be worth hiring someone else to do.

Emotional issues may continue to cause problems with your co-parent as you nest. After all these years, Bill and I do get along pretty well and may spend more time together than most nesters. I don't think this was either of our original plans—we were getting *divorced*, after all—but circumstances (see the Covid shutdown and our kids home from school; Bill's work travel being placed on hold) resulted in us spending a lot more time together than we originally planned. Also, we have—with a lot of hard work on both our parts—resolved, or at least addressed, most of our lingering emotional issues with each other. But it is certainly possible to nest with a lot more separation than we have. Both Kate and her ex and Michael and his—and many other nesting families—only briefly interact in person with each other in the nest at transition time.

If you struggle with challenging emotions from the end of your marriage or if you find that issues from your relationship are exacerbated by co-parenting and nesting, you can make a point—in coordination with your ex, if possible—of gradually limiting the amount of time that you need to interact with each other. This will get easier to do as you hit your stride in terms of the logistics and scheduling side of nesting.

Also, if you had a therapist while you were setting up nesting, you may want to keep that relationship going—even if it's just on an as-needed basis. The first year or so after our divorce, I continued to meet with my therapist regularly, but scheduled appointments farther apart as time went on. Eventually, we switched to meeting only when I felt I needed to see her. Sometimes I'll go six months without consulting with her; sometimes just a couple of weeks. While topics of conversation have evolved beyond those early years, when it was all about the divorce and the challenges of nesting co-parenting, I still, on occasion, seek her help to sort through a parenting or co-parenting challenge. (Note: If you don't already have a long-term relationship with a therapist and are beginning with a new one, you may not be able to establish a flexible schedule of therapy right away—they may ask for more regular meetings at first. This is certainly a question you should ask if you are looking for a new therapist.)

UNANTICIPATED HURDLES

Sometimes the circumstances that almost everyone experiences at some point in life can impact your nesting situation, such as social, mental, or other health issues; the loss of a loved one; or caring for aging or ailing parents.

Of course, long- or short-term illness—your own, your ex's, or your kids'—may require one of you to pick up more of the parenting slack, temporarily become the other one's caregiver, or modify your living arrangements for a while.

Ours are relatively minor compared to health issues others may have had to deal with, but I'll give some examples. Bill recently had foot surgery and had to stay off his feet and not drive for two weeks. I came into the house for a few days right after his surgery to do the parenting, dog, and house stuff, and—thank goodness!—his girlfriend came to stay to take care of him, get his prescriptions, and drive him to doctors' appointments. For me, Bill has had to cancel work travel when I've been hit by the flu and had to check out of parenting for a few days. And Covid hit our household in the summer of 2022. Fortunately, Bill and the boys weren't terribly sick and stayed in the house to recover. I lived at my apartment (and didn't get sick), but I stopped by the house every day to water the landscaping and take care of the pool, and to leave groceries or whatever else they needed in the garage.

When we have had more stressful health events to deal with, I have always been comforted by the fact that my children were in a nesting situation—rather than shuttling back and forth between two different houses—as we went through them. Being based in one house also made it easier for Bill and me to adapt to whatever was needed. There was a very frightening time when one of our sons was in a hospital in Chicago for almost a month and had two major surgeries while he was there. (He's completely fine now.) I stayed at the hospital with him most of the time while Bill kept the home fires burning and everything consistent for our two other boys. Of course, his brothers were worried, but I often thought, *Thank good-ness they are in the comfort of their home and in their regular routine as Bill and I try to deal with all of this!*

I had similar thoughts when my father—with whom my boys were very close—passed away and we were all grieving the loss. I was also very busy and distracted as I helped my mom with everything that needed doing. It was such a comfort to me to know the kids were with their dad, in their home (and they had their dog to snuggle with), day in, day out, and Bill could keep their routine as consistent as possible. Nesting doesn't take away fear or grief, of course, but I wouldn't have traded the extra bit of comfort and consistency it brought during those rough times for anything.

DATING AND INTRODUCING NEW PARTNERS

You may be interested in starting to date, now that nesting is feeling more settled. Dating can take a lot of time and emotional energy. To start, it's best to schedule your dating time—and time on the apps—outside of your parenting time in the nest. As licensed counselor Réa Wright advises, "You should work around the kids' schedule. Date when you are on your own, not when you are on parenting duty."

If you've begun dating, you may have experienced that dating as a nester can present some challenges. The primary one is explaining nesting to a date—to someone you barely know. As noted in chapter 7, "Telling Family and Friends—Step Four," nesting is still a rather uncommon situation and can be met with doubt or confusion by those unfamiliar with it. Dating after divorce is hard enough; adding an explanation of nesting to the first date-night agenda can make it seem even more daunting. Personally, though, I found it a quick way to weed out who was worth continuing to share my time with. I always thought it best to bring up the nesting situation on the first date, as soon as it was relevant to the conversation. Not to bring it up at all seemed duplicitous, and delaying telling someone seemed to indicate that I was embarrassed by the situation—which I most certainly was not. Also, it establishes right away that your children are your priority. I was only interested in dating someone who could appreciate that.

That said, because of the relative rarity of nesting, it may be reasonable for your date to wonder—either out loud or to themselves—if nesting means you are trying to get back with your ex. In explaining nesting, you should be very clear that you and your ex's romantic relationship is over; you are co-parenting by nesting because you think it is best for your children. Then, of course, your actions and words on future dates should continue to signal that you are interested in *this* person, not trying to reconcile with your ex. (If you *are* hoping to reconcile with your ex, you probably should not be dating. Work that issue out on your own or with a neutral party like a therapist before you involve someone else in your unresolved issues.)

Not everyone will understand, even after a few dates, however. Suzanne notes an issue she has encountered in dating as a nesting mom: "The man will accept that I live this way right now but can't accept that I intend to continue to do it. They wonder how they will fit in. Or they want me to change my situation and come 'play happy family' at their house, which wouldn't be fair to my kids."

Depending on the person you are dating, issues like this could be worked out with open conversations. Or not. In which case, they probably are not the right person for you.

Dating later in life does limit your pool of options and presents different challenges (and "baggage") than when you were younger. If you are looking to be in a new relationship, it may take time to find someone who understands why nesting is right for you and your family, and who is willing to be patient about learning how to fit into your family's nesting arrangement. Don't lose hope: Many of the nesters I have come to know are happily in new relationships, and even remarried.

As Lauren recalls, "My first partner after the separation did not have kids and didn't really understand that I wanted to wait to integrate her into the boys' lives. This was the main reason we split up. Also, my ex didn't like her and didn't want her to be in the nest. But now everyone loves my new partner and she's fully integrated into our family."

Others—and I would count myself among these—enjoy the distinction between "parenting time" and "dating and relationship time" that divorce and nesting provide.

Kate explains, "I met someone a few years after my relationship with my ex ended. My new partner and I were, and are, very committed to each other. But, early on, I had no intention of embedding him in our family. I was living two very separate lives and I loved that about my life. I think I was built for part-time mothering and part-time relationship."

There will come a time when you have met the right person and you want to introduce them to your children. (In chapters 4 and 6, we discuss why it is best to hold off on introducing dating partners to the kids.) This person will hopefully be a wonderful addition to your children's lives, but there is no need to rush the process. Even though you are nesting, your children are dealing with the big change of their parents no longer being a couple. Allow them time to process the new family dynamic, and to enjoy lots of one-on-one time with you.

Wright, the licensed counselor, advises, "Do not introduce your kids until you are sure this relationship is going to be a long-term commitment. It is hard for kids to have people coming in and out of their lives. They can worry they are losing a parent when someone new comes into the picture."

Communicating about this with your ex is important as well. Licensed therapist Holly Rothenbush recommends two initial steps to take when you feel ready to introduce your new partner: "First, both parents should talk to each other about how they will talk to the kids about dating. Then one or both of you should have a conversation with the kids about dating in general, not yet about introducing the new person. You're not asking your kids if it's okay for you to date—because, of course, it's okay for you to want to date. But you are giving them a chance to tell you their feelings about it. Ask, listen, and validate how they feel."

How the children react to the general topic of dating will help you gauge how ready they are to be introduced to a new partner. You may need to revisit the dating conversation a couple of times to help them get comfortable with the idea. It's probably best not to push them to talk, just bring it up casually until they get more comfortable, or bored, when you bring it up.

Wright suggests that once you feel the kids are ready to meet the new person in your life, you can "introduce the new person as a 'friend' and do it in little ways, like lunch together or a hike." The point is to allow your children to get to know your new significant other slowly, to give them time to adjust.

Suzanne recalls that her ex introduced their kids to his new girlfriend, now his wife, about six months after they began dating.

"Ana was described at first as Papa's 'friend.' It was a good icebreaker that the kids met her dog at that first meeting, too."

As for me, after I had been dating my boyfriend for about eight months, I felt the time had come for my kids to get to know him. First, I talked through with my therapist how this process might work. She suggested bringing up the topic of dating in general first, before talking about a specific person, and to think of a neutral place or activity for them all to meet.

I let Bill know that I wanted to introduce Fred to the kids. I was very nervous about that conversation! Bill and I were aware that the other person was dating—but we hadn't really talked about it yet, and he didn't yet know how committed I felt to Fred.

Bill and I agreed with my therapist's suggestion that I should start by having a conversation with the kids just about dating in general, to mention to them that, now that we were divorced, Dad and I might start dating at some point.

Next, I spoke to the boys one evening at dinner about how Dad and I would probably start dating now that we'd been divorced a while—how did they feel about that? The oldest shrugged and said, "You're adults." The other two nodded. I didn't exactly *press* them on their feelings about it . . . just figured if I wasn't sensing any shock or sadness, they were fine. I also mentioned to their therapist that I had brought this topic up with the boys and asked her to please keep an ear out for any stress this might be causing them.

Next, I told Fred that I would like him to meet my kids—was he ready for that? The reason I talked to Fred after I had talked to Bill and my kids was that I didn't want him to start anticipating meeting my kids before I knew if Bill and the boys were okay with it. Fred was happy to have a chance to get to know my kids, and we decided that dinner at the boys' favorite sushi restaurant would work well. I liked the idea of meeting at a restaurant because it was neutral territory, there would be the distraction of food, and there is a set end point when you are eating out.

A couple of weeks after the general dating conversation, I brought up to the boys that I had a friend I'd been seeing a lot of lately and I would really like them to meet him. I told them we'd be going to their favorite restaurant, so they were excited about that.

It came off really well! I was so proud of all of them! Fred has a son (we'd agreed to introduce our kids to each other at a later time) so he knew how to talk to kids. My boys were fourteen, eleven, and seven at the time—still young, but old enough to know to answer politely and to ask questions about the other person. It was a very pleasant evening. I kind of figured it would be fine, but it was nice to get it behind me!

A few notes on some specifics of the evening. Perhaps I was overthinking things (who, me?!), but they were important to me at the time and I'm still glad I made these seemingly small choices:

+ I drove the boys and myself from our house and back, rather than having Fred pick us up. He just met us at the restaurant. I wanted to send the message to my kids that I was in charge of the evening: "I, your mother, am with you. I'm going home with you."

+ After the boys were introduced and shook hands, Fred and I had just a very brief hug, no kissy-face. I didn't want to creep the kids out.

+ The real stroke of genius? I brought a pen and notepad to dinner for us to play hangman. It took the pressure off all of us to make conversation while we waited for our food (and—mom-brag—was a subtle way to impress Fred with what an excellent vocabulary my children have).

+ I paid for everyone. Again, in my mind, to send the message, "I, your mother, am taking care of this."

+ Fred walked us to our car. Handshakes for the boys and a very quick hug for me. I thanked the kids on the drive home, but we didn't dwell on it. Just another dinner out.

I was fortunate that the initial meeting went well and that gradually and over time, my kids got to know Fred better and that they all get along. If your initial meeting doesn't go as well as you'd hoped, I would suggest holding off on future meetings until you have had time to discuss with your therapist, and your kids' therapist, if possible, how it went and what was disappointing to you. Getting your kids' reactions—if you feel they can honestly talk to you about this topic—can give you some insight as well. You can continue to date this new person, but it may be best to hold off on bringing them all together again until you have a handle on why the first meeting didn't go as well as you'd hoped.

It helps if *both* parents make it known to the kids that they feel comfortable with the other parent dating. Jean recalls, "We were accepting of what the other person was doing. We also were coming from a place of 'anything is possible' and not hating the other person—we still liked each other. And milestones, like dating someone new, meant that new person would be invited to dinner and feel accepted. We believed that approach was best for the kids."

An important milestone in your nesting may be when that new person becomes a more official part of the family. Suzanne says her ex remarrying wasn't a problem for her because "my kids gained a third parent who loves them. They get all of their parents in one place, which means more time with each of us. Plus, they don't have to shuffle themselves back and forth between houses. For the kids it's always been a total win."

Cooperative and supportive exes are certainly a plus, but the openness of the new person matters as well. As Lauren says, "My new partner is the reason bringing her into the family has worked so well. She is so loving with my sons. It helps that she has her own kids and has gone through her own divorce, so she fully understands the situation and is very open to whatever arrangements work for my kids."

Lauren also credits nesting itself with helping to integrate her new partner into the family: "I honestly think that nesting not only helped our kids weather the separation with very little emotional distress, but it also helped our family stay a family. We really feel like one big extended family now," she says. "In fact, when my new partner and I got married, my ex and our kids held the chuppah [the Jewish wedding canopy] for us! We had a small family ceremony in my parents' backyard. It was wonderful."

Bill and I have been fortunate to each find partners who are supportive of nesting and our commitment to our kids.

Over these past six years, Fred and I have continued growing our relationship and spending lots of time together when neither of us were with our children. While I wanted my kids to know that he is an important part of my life, I didn't think it was necessary for him to become a big part of *their* lives when they were young. They have their dad in their lives already, and Fred has his own son to focus on.

But over time our kids have definitely become comfortable with Fred (and Terri, Bill's partner) often being around. They each occasionally have dinner at our house and sometimes (depending on their schedules with their own families) have been included in our family's frequent celebrations and holiday traditions.

When to Transition Out of Nesting

Even the most positive nesting experience won't last forever. The kids will leave home *eventually*, right? That's a definite reason for wrapping up longer-term nesting: the last little birdie is leaving the nest, maybe for college or moving on to pursue their own life. But there is no hard and fast rule that you have to stick with it until then. There are lots of reasons co-parents may decide that nesting is no longer the best option for their family—whether that's a new job, a remarriage, or a change in financial situation. It is still a great accomplishment that you nested for whatever length of time that helped your children and made sense for you and your ex.

Just as starting up nesting took some planning and work, wrapping it up successfully will require this as well. As always, prioritizing the needs of your kids, thinking creatively, and communicating openly with your ex will bring you the greatest success in this process.

If either of you thinks the time for bringing nesting to an end has come, the first thing to do is to have a conversation with your co-parent.

Here are some questions to consider:

+ What is the date by which we want to be done with
  nesting, and is that date realistic?
+ What do we each envision for how and where we will live
  after nesting ends?
+ What needs to happen logistically to bring nesting to an end?
+ Are there legal or financial issues we need to address when
  nesting ends, and with which professionals?

If you will still be co-parenting—i.e., your children will begin
moving between you and your ex's two residences—give particular
attention to how the end of nesting will impact the children. These are
questions to discuss with your co-parent to help the kids transition to
their new living situation as easily as possible:

+ What issues will the end of nesting present for our kids?
+ What changes can they expect?
+ What can we do to make the transition as easy as possible
  for them?
+ When will we, together, talk with the children about
  this change?
+ What are our agreed-upon talking points when presenting
  the news to our children? (For instance, When will the

change happen? What specifically will change for them and what will stay the same?)

+ Which legal and financial issues do we need to address before nesting ends and which professionals do we need to help us?

Steps to Transition Out of Nesting

With prompting from the questions above, you can next determine the steps that need to be taken in terms of housing, finances, and logistics. First and foremost, consider how these changes may impact your children.

As you plan out your steps, consider if and how the children might be involved. The ages of your children can help you decide how much information they are capable of handling, similar to the guidelines in chapter 5 "Talking to Your Children About Divorce and Nesting." For example, telling a younger child that you are thinking about ending nesting before you have a plan in place may cause them anxiety. They will want to understand as soon as possible what will be changing for them in their own daily life. When you and your ex have the first conversation with younger children, it's best to have some specifics to share with them. Remember to give them plenty of advance warning before changes begin and to continue to explain the next steps before they happen.

Therapist Holly Rothenbush recommends, "It's still important to communicate—*together*—what you are considering for the next stage. Even if your kids are now older, it can be similar to the divorce conversation you had with them when you began nesting. It's important to be open, that both parents are talking with them, and—even though it is ultimately your decision—to let your kids know that you want to hear their thoughts and feelings."

An older child, say one who can drive themself or is looking at going away to college or moving out soon, will likely be less upset by a discussion about how nesting will be ending. They may even enjoy being part of the process as their parents look for new places to live. Still, respect their role as a member of the family by giving them plenty of advance warning before changes begin, and encourage them to share their thoughts and feelings with you. Even though they may be looking forward to moving into their own life, they may also feel sad about the loss of their childhood home.

SELLING THE NEST

There are so many steps to selling a home. To start, you should set a hoped-for selling date and then work backward from that to outline specific tasks (kind of like when you were setting up nesting, as discussed in chapter 4, "Agreeing to Nest with Your Spouse/

Soon-to-Be-Ex—Step One). Some of the work may require hiring professionals, like a Realtor, home repair or upgrade contractors, or movers. Some of the work you'll likely tackle yourself, like going through and dividing up the household items and furniture. There are the financials of the sale to consider as well. You may have predetermined these in your settlement agreement, or you may want to revisit this issue with your attorney. Deborah Lansing, the Realtor in Montclair, New Jersey, says, "It can be an unexpected problem when one person gets saddled with selling the house and has to absorb all the costs and fees associated with that."

FINDING NEW HOMES

You can tackle some of these yourself, but you may want to bring a Realtor on board to assist in finding new residences and hiring movers to transition to your new spaces. You may also need to revisit your settlement agreement with your attorney to determine if the financials still apply to your new arrangement, including if child support needs to be adjusted in light of changed housing costs.

FINANCES

If you will still be co-parenting you will probably need to revisit the settlement or child support agreements. If you have been sharing a bank account to support the nest, it may make sense to end this arrangement, or to revise parameters of the account—and your budget—to support only child-related costs.

If you will no longer be co-parenting, other aspects of your financial situation will likely change as the nest is sold. You may want to seek professional guidance from your accountant or financial adviser. Ron Carboni, financial planner, says, "Your planner could talk over with you how your financial needs will change after you end nesting. You may need to make some adjustments to prepare for, or benefit from, the end of co-parenting. If you will own the home together or still share financial accounts, a financial adviser could help you figure out how to divide those, if it wasn't already determined in your settlement agreement. They can coordinate with your accountant or attorney, too, to help you set yourself up well for the next stage."

Considering the above questions and steps should help you develop your plan for ending nesting. Or they might lead you to decide that perhaps you aren't quite ready to do all that work to bring nesting to an end. Because it *is* work.

Bill and I actually considered ending nesting about two and a half years after we had begun. Sure, in the early days after the divorce, calling it quits sometimes came up in the heat of an argument, then fizzled out once our tempers cooled. However, in 2016, for a variety of reasons, we were seriously talking about it. He was dealing with stress and uncertainty in his career and dating relationship.

I was dealing with him being stressed out. It was affecting our co-parenting and causing each of us to wonder if nesting might be adding more stress to our lives than it was worth.

But how to end it in our situation? All three kids were still at home and not old enough to drive themselves yet. We had the nest. I had the apartment. And Bill was gone half the month traveling for work.

Going to a traditional two-home, kids-with-each-parent 50/50 raised several big questions for us. Did it make financial sense for Bill to keep the family home (with a large yard and a swimming pool to maintain) when the kids were only there half the time? When he traveled for work, who would take care of it, as I had been doing? Hiring yard, landscape, and pool companies would be expensive.

The one-bedroom apartment I was living in when I was not in the nest wasn't large enough to house our three kids and all their stuff. I either needed to find a larger space, ideally one that was still convenient to their school and their friends and activities, or I needed to buy Bill out of the house and take over maintaining it. I couldn't cover that on my freelance writing income, so we would have to readjust the divorce settlement. *Or* I'd need to find a higher-paying, full-time job—but that created all sorts of childcare complications and increased costs.

If Bill moved out of the house, he would need to find another place to live, with the same space and location considerations I would need to consider. And—what?—I would just sit in that big house by myself for half the month while the boys were at his place— *not* enjoying their yard and pool, and their friends in the neighborhood? What if we both just got two smaller houses? Who wants to tell the kids they can't stay in the comfortable house they grew up in anymore?

If we were going with the two smaller houses route, we'd need to sell the family home. We already knew it needed a new roof. What other repairs would have to be done to a seventy-year-old house before it could be put on the market?

We'd also have to pay attorneys to redo the divorce settlement to adjust for changing housing-related finances, to reevaluate childcare and child support financials, and so many other aspects of our legal agreement. How—and *when*—would any of that lead each of us to better financial situations?

Here's where our experience may differ from most couples discussing ending nesting (or maybe not). Bill knew he wanted to end nesting and had a date in mind: by the start of the new year, so the kids could be in the nest for Christmas. I did not particularly want to end nesting, but I also didn't want to stay in a situation that was making both of us so stressed out. I had given a lot of thought to what it would entail to end nesting and figure out a new situation.

We'd agreed to meet in person at the nest to start hashing it all out. I'd asked my parents to take the kids out to dinner for a couple of hours because I didn't want the boys to have the slightest idea we were thinking about ending nesting, not until we had a preliminary plan in place to tell them.

It was a beautiful early fall evening and Bill suggested that we sit on the front porch to begin our talk. We both hemmed and hawed and struggled with where to start the discussion. My brain felt like it was stuck in one of those Escher drawings where every staircase leads nowhere. Finally, I just launched into my list of questions and talking points—very similar to those listed above—and I saw Bill grow pensive.

"You know who is going to suffer if we end nesting?" said Bill. "The boys."

"Right," I nodded.

"Maybe we can figure out *some* way to make it better," he said. "And keep everything the same for them. Let's table this for now . . ."

Now, I don't know for certain what Bill was thinking. I'm sure there was partly a selfless realization that he didn't want to upend the consistency of our kids' lives. But I also wondered if maybe he just hadn't fully realized how much work—with a questionable amount of payoff—he was getting himself into if he really wanted to end nesting.

What I did see after that meeting was Bill shift his energies into addressing the stresses from his job and his relationship, instead of complaining about the challenges of nesting. Personally, I realized that I would have much better results in nesting if I straight-on addressed issues rather than feeling stressed out and just focusing on getting out of the situation. (Yes, I know this is a good approach to *life*, too. I'm working on it.)

What I do know is this: From that moment on, there was a shift. We were both fully committed to nesting—that is, our children—being the priority in our lives. Finances, careers, other relationships could all be figured out around that constant.

But nesting *will* end for us someday. I look to these examples from two of our nesting families to help me think about how we might approach it ourselves.

Lauren still had a child at home when she and her ex decided to end nesting. Her older son had left for college. Lauren says, "Nesting had been going really well, but we took a look at our situation and realized that the boys didn't really need nesting so much anymore, and we really needed money to pay for college."

In January 2020 they decided to put their nest on the market and began renovations—until the pandemic hit in March and everything shut down. Lauren is a front-line caregiver. At the beginning of the pandemic, they decided it was best for her ex, who was now working from home, to move in with their sons and for Lauren to live full time with her new partner, and not go to the nest at all, as she continued working.

"Ultimately, I started 'visiting' the boys in the nest, but at that point my ex had moved in with them full time and it really did not feel like my place anymore," recalls Lauren. "I was living full time in the Bronx and visiting the boys in Brooklyn when I could. That was just not working for me."

Fortunately, the pandemic had made rents quite low in Brooklyn and Lauren and her new partner were able to find a large apartment not far from the nest. The son who was still at home started spending half the week with them and half with his other mom back at the nest.

As luck would have it, just as the nest sold, an apartment became available in the same building as Lauren's. Her ex now lives one floor down and their son spends half the week with Lauren and half with his other mom.

Lauren says, "He comes up and down whenever he wants. My ex and my new partner have become very close, and we have family dinners at least once a week. Sometimes I come home from work and find them all hanging out on the couch! So, we aren't really nesting anymore, but it almost feels like we are."

Another scenario might be hanging on to the nest longer than the parents may have originally intended—through college or even after it—which may offer opportunities for both parents and kids to segue more smoothly into their next stages of life.

Tedd and Jean's older child has graduated from college, moved back home for work, and pays them rent to stay in the nest. Their daughter was still in college when this happened, but Tedd and Jean could foresee that nesting would not be required for their kids for much longer. There were other factors that moved them closer to ending nesting: Jean's mother had died and her house (the space Tedd and Jean had been living in during their off-duty parenting time) was sold. Additionally, Tedd changed careers and began traveling extensively. "My new job helped alleviate the shared-living situation because I'm rarely home," says Tedd. Jean moved full time into the family home. When Tedd is in town, he stays with his girlfriend. Jean and Tedd plan to put their home on the market soon.

"I don't feel sad about leaving the house," says Jean. "I feel less of a special bond to it than I used to. That feeling was more driven by it being the kids' home. I may or may not even stay in our town after the house sells. We'll see."

When Bill and I first started nesting, we were often asked, "How long are you going to do it?" Our reply was, "As long as it makes sense." Because we didn't know. And we still don't—at least when it comes down to specifics. It's been nice to still be in the family home when the oldest comes home from college. The middle one will leave for college in a year. It seems like it would *still* be nice for him to come home from college. The youngest still has high school ahead of him. It's too soon to say if we will definitely sell the nest when he leaves for college. There are a lot of moving parts to each of our lives, plus unknown factors that will surely arise, that we will need to consider before making that decision.

Bill and I have talked about different options and considerations for the future. In the course of writing this book, Bill and Terri got engaged and married soon after. Fred and I also have gotten engaged, but we don't have a definite timeline yet for when our marriage will take place.

Before Bill and I let the kids know the good news about our engagements, we discussed with each other some of our ideas for the future. Of course, there will be changes, but as Bill points out, "*Every* change you choose to make in life should be gradual. And the more drastic the change, the longer it should take."

When we shared our happy news with our three boys, who were twenty-one, eighteen, and fourteen at the time, we said—as we said *all those years ago* when we sat around the same dining room table and first told them about our divorce and nesting: "But right now nothing is changing for you. This is still your home and we are still a family."

IN BRIEF: DOWN THE ROAD

Challenges are bound to arise as you continue nesting, either from ongoing issues or unanticipated changes. These may include:

+ Careers or financial situations
+ Health issues or loss of loved ones

But mainly, longer-term nesting is about daily life being the same, happening rather unremarkably without any missteps related to nesting. Regularly remind yourself of the results of your efforts and take a moment to fully enjoy them.

The need to transition out of nesting may occur due to a number of challenges and milestones:

+ Changes for either of you: new job, remarriage, or a change in financial situation
+ Changes for the children: leaving the nest to head to college or pursue other goals

You or your ex may wish to start dating, and eventually introduce your new partner to your children. It's important not to rush the process.

+ Don't introduce your children to your new partner until you are certain you're in a long-term relationship
+ Talk to your ex about how both of you will discuss dating and new relationships with your children, so you're on the same page
+ Let your children have the opportunity to tell you how they feel about dating in general, not yet about meeting a specific person
+ Give your children the time they need to get to know the new person, and don't force it

When your or your ex feels it's time to transition, come to an agreement of what that might mean. Life after nesting, especially if you are still co-parenting, may involve revisions to your divorce agreement and your financial arrangements, which may include eliminating shared bank accounts or selling your home. Once you have a clear picture of what life will look like after nesting, discuss the plan with your kids—*together*.

Conclusion:
Changing the Future
of Families and Divorce

As my children are getting older and closer to adulthood, I still wonder how—or even if—Bill's and my decision to nest affected their emotional development or outlooks on life. Sometimes I do get some insight, though, and often in unexpected ways.

Our middle child is entering his senior year of high school, so we've had college on our minds a lot lately. He's supposed to be working on his "Common App" essay (the Common Application is a single form that kids use to apply to a whole bunch of colleges, instead of doing a separate form for each school, as in the olden days when I went to college). The college counselors at his school sent home some writing prompts to help the kids brainstorm their essay ideas. I'm immediately drawn to anything that has to do with writing, so I was reading through the packet over my breakfast cereal. The prompts included a list of a hundred words from which the kids were supposed to circle five to ten that described themselves or their interests. He had not done the exercise himself (no, I was not surprised), but I grabbed a piece of scrap paper and made a list of words that I thought described him: untraditional, creative, curious, history, family.

In that moment, I had a revelation. "Not only do those describe Mick, they are also at the heart of what nesting is all about. He's grown up immersed in our choice to nest. Perhaps that has in some way influenced who he is today."

And—as only a mom can—I genuinely thought, "I'll bet he would appreciate my insight and would find it helpful in framing his essay."

I imagined that his response might be, "Thanks for the helpful suggestion, Mom. That's an interesting idea." (I *know*. You'd think I'd have learned by now.)

Later, I brought up my idea to him and did *not* get thanks and appreciation. Instead, he impatiently responded: "If *you* want to write a Common App essay on nesting, go right ahead." His tone said, *Why am I burdened with a mother who is so lame?*

"It was just a suggestion!" I responded. "You don't have to be snarky!"

"Mom, I don't think you realize how little your and Dad's divorce impacted my life. Like, *not at all*," he said with a dramatic sigh.

For a moment, my feelings were hurt, I must admit. Then a slow realization came over me: This was the greatest compliment I had ever received.

Our decision to nest has led him to feel—as he clearly stated— that our divorce had no impact on him at all.

Maybe, someday, as more and more of us choose nesting, most kids will only roll their eyes when someone suggests the trauma of their parents' divorce left them bruised for life. Maybe the snide remarks made about how adult children of divorce spend all their money on therapy will become obsolete and make absolutely no sense anymore. We can only hope.

Through a conscious divorce, you demonstrate to your children that they will always come first. You will teach them invaluable lessons about the importance of family, the value of forgiveness and moving past mistakes, and how working constructively with other people can help get you through difficult times. You have modeled for them how love and life can evolve, and sometimes a family can evolve to be even better than it was before. Those are lessons that will stay with your children the rest of their lives, and positively influence their own future choices and relationships.

You may have found that nesting led you to a better relationship with your ex, better than it ever was before. Nesting can unburden the parents of the effort to try to keep their marriage working and allow them to transition into a new and different relationship. Where many have chosen to hang on to anger and resentment after divorce—or even stay unhappily married—you are choosing patience and acceptance. You choose to honor what came out of the experience of being a couple and express your gratitude for it by focusing on one of the most important outcomes of your time together—your children.

When I divorced in 2014, very few attorneys were familiar with nesting, and the courts even less so. The attorneys and mediators I spoke to for this book all had experience with nesting arrangements and told me that judges are familiar with the concept and increasingly implementing nesting as a temporary measure. The more attorneys, mediators, and judges who are familiar with nesting, the easier it will be for creative arrangements—that benefit the entire family—to be implemented. But that push ultimately needs to come from us, the divorcing parents. We are parents who don't want to be boxed into the traditional approach, and who are willing to work with each other and with professionals to explore and implement positive, creative co-parenting solutions like nesting. Parents who truly want to put their children first.

Nesting is a crucial part of a larger sea change movement in our society to divorce differently. As more and more families refuse to embrace the status quo of divorce, those "micro-changes" will add up. And that's how society evolves and improves. We are affecting the world by *proving* that another model—one rooted in positivity and love—can be the answer. I encourage you to share your own nesting stories with others, to help and inspire them, to show that the divorces of the past don't have to be our guideposts anymore. Anyone can—and should—pursue their own creative path to divorce in a kinder, gentler way, and to honor their family's past and celebrate its future.

Acknowledgments

I am so grateful to the nesting parents who willingly and openly shared their personal experiences. All of them expressed their hope that sharing their stories could help other parents find their own way to nesting. I don't doubt that their advice and insights will be encouraging to countless others. Thanks as well to the professionals who offered their valuable perspectives on navigating the practical aspects of nesting.

This book wouldn't exist if my agent, Liz Kracht of Kimberley Cameron & Associates, hadn't believed in its message and never lost faith that its time would come. Her help was invaluable in finding it just the right home. Immense thanks to my editor, Jessica Firger at Union Square & Co., who encouraged me to dig deep and develop my thoughts in ways I never would have gotten to on my own. I am so grateful for her help and guidance (and that she laughed in all the right spots).

I am thankful for Christina and Beth, who encouraged me from the first days of my wondering, *Maybe I could be a writer?* They've proofread countless things over the years (how lucky am I that my best friends are not only brilliant and funny, but also great writers?), and were the first ones with whom I shared the tiny seed of an idea for this book. Their advice and support helped it develop and grow, and all the talks and laughs we've shared through this process have helped keep me going.

With love to Fred, my steady and never-tiring source of support and happiness every day and through every bit of this book-writing journey. I love you and am so very excited for our future together.

To Bill. I will always be grateful for all of it. From Chapel Hill to Capitol Hill and all the adventures in between and since—including our most rewarding adventure: parenting together our three great kids.

Words can't fully express my boundless love and gratitude to Jack, Mick, and Max for the best hugs, the laughter (even when it's at my expense), and for each of your individual and intelligent perspectives from which I continue to learn so much. I am so very, very lucky to get to be your mom.

Further Reading and Resources

I turned to many books and resources as I began to consider divorce and nesting. Thankfully, there is so much more information available now, both online and in print, but you will probably find it's impossible for just one resource to provide all the answers you need. You'll likely have to piece information together from a variety of places, but here are the resources I found most helpful to get you started.

You can contact me through my websites FamilyNesting.Org and BethBehrendt .Com, and connect with other nesters through our Facebook group, Family Nesting.

Books

DIVORCE AND CO-PARENTING

Kindlon, Dan, and Michael Thompson. *Raising Cain, Protecting the Emotional Life of Boys.* Ballantine Books, 2000.

Hazlewood, Toby. *Bird-nesting: Extreme Coparenting After Divorce.* Self-published, 2018.

Pedro-Carroll, Joanne. *Putting Children First: Proven Parenting Strategies for Helping Children Thrive Through Divorce.* Avery, 2010.

Wasser, Laura. *It Doesn't Have to Be That Way: How to Divorce Without Destroying Your Family or Bankrupting Yourself.* St. Martin's Griffin, 2014.

You can read more about our nester Suzanne's story in her book:

Vickberg, Suzanne. *Divorce by Design: What if Staying or Leaving Aren't Your Only Options.* Suzanne Vickberg LLC, 2023.

FINANCES

Landers, Jeffrey A. *A Woman's Guide to Financial Security After Divorce: The Basics: Creating A Solid Foundation (Think Financially, Not Emotionally® Book 3).* Sourced Media Books, 2015.

Woodhouse, Violet P., and Lina Guillen, Attorney. *Divorce & Money: Make the Best Financial Decisions During Divorce.* NOLO, 2019.

PERSONAL DEVELOPMENT

Brown, Brené. *The Gifts of Imperfection: Let Go of Who You Think You're Supposed to Be and Embrace Who You Are.* Hazelden Publishing, 2012.

Cameron, Julia. *The Artist's Way.* TarcherPerigee, 1986.

Tawwab, Nedra Glover. *Set Boundaries, Find Peace: A Guide to Reclaiming Yourself.* TarcherPerigee, 2021.

Tolle, Eckhart. *The Power of Now.* New World Library, 2004.

FOR CHILDREN

CHILDREN AGES FIVE AND UNDER

Books that may help to explain nesting to your little ones:

Hurley, Jorey. *Nest (Classic Board Books).* Little Simon, 2015.

Stemple, Heidi E. Y. *Whose Nest Is Best?: A Lift-the-Flap Book Board.* Little Simon 2022.

CHILDREN SIX AND OVER

Brown, Marc, and Laurie Krasney Brown. *Dinosaurs Divorce*. Little Brown, 1988.

Heegaard, Marge. *When Mom and Dad Separate: Children Can Learn to Cope with Grief from Divorce*. Woodland Press, 1996.

Schab, Lisa M. *The Divorce Workbook for Children*. Instant Help, 2008.

Online Resources for Divorce, Nesting, Co-Parenting, and Therapy-Related Information

Divorce Magazine, www.divorcemag.com.

Parents Magazine, www.parents.com/parenting/divorce/.

Psychology Today, psychologytoday.com.

Survive Divorce: Divorce Advice Laws and Resources, www.survivedivorce.com

The Connecticut Council for Non-Adversarial Divorce, gooddivorcect.com (includes information of relevance beyond just Connecticut)

The Library of Congress has compiled a list of the best books for beginners on divorce and law:

Family Law: A Beginner's Guide. Library of Congress, 2021. https://guides.loc.gov/family-law/marriage-divorce/books.

Podcasts

Divorcing Well: The Podcast with Leanne Townsend

The Divorce and Beyond Podcast with Susan Guthrie

The Good Divorce Podcast with Tom Hendrick

Sources

Chapter 1 Two-Home Conventional Divorce and Its Traumatic Effects

page 14: *Even through the 1960s . . . mothers were, by and large, the default primary caregivers*: Giulia M. Dotti Sani and Judith Treas, "Educational Gradients in Parents' Child-Care Time Across Countries, 1965–2012," *Journal of Marriage and Family* 78, no. 4 (April 19, 2016): 1083–1096, https://doi.org/10.1111/jomf.12305.

page 15: *Judith Wallerstein reports disturbing trends in her groundbreaking study*: Judith Wallerstein, Julia M. Lewis, and Sandra Blakeslee, *The Unexpected Legacy of Divorce: The 25 Year Landmark Study* (New York: Hyperion, 2000).

page 21: *The role of parents . . . is to create as supportive and safe a place as possible*: Judith Wallerstein, Julia M. Lewis, and Sandra Blakeslee, *The Unexpected Legacy of Divorce: The 25 Year Landmark Study* (New York: Hyperion, 2000).

page 22: *Experts say that the age of the children at the time of the divorce predicts many of the behaviors they will likely exhibit*: Judith Wallerstein, Julia M. Lewis, and Sandra Blakeslee, *The Unexpected Legacy of Divorce: The 25 Year Landmark Study* (New York: Hyperion, 2000).

page 24: *Wallerstein's study finds that another common change in the parent-child dynamic after a broken-home divorce is that a child may feel that he or she needs to move* into a caregiver role with one or both parents: Judith Wallerstein, Julia M. Lewis, and Sandra Blakeslee, *The Unexpected Legacy of Divorce: The 25 Year Landmark Study.* (New York: Hyperion, 2000).

Chapter 2: A New and Better Way—Nesting

page 39: *A 2018 study, published in the Journal of School Health, reports that of over four hundred early adolescents (grades 4–7), those with a positive self-image had the strongest overall emotional well-being—even more so than children who had lots of friends or did well in school:* Eva Oberle. PhD, "Early Adolescents' Emotional Well-Being in the Classroom: The Role of Personal and Contextual Assets," *Journal of School Health* 88, no. 2 (January, 14 2018): 101–111, https://doi.org/10.1111/josh.12585.

page 41: *The researchers who wrote* The Unexpected Legacy of Divorce: The 25 Year Landmark Study *comment that one of the saddest of their findings was that the children of two-home divorces did not feel a sense of continuity with the family history:* Judith Wallerstein, Julia M. Lewis, and Sandra Blakeslee, *The Unexpected Legacy of Divorce: The 25 Year Landmark Study* (New York: Hyperion, 2000).

page 44: *Researchers from Emory University reported in their 2018 study . . . that children were more emotionally healthy when their parents shared personal stories with them about coping with stress, anger, or sadness:* Natalie Merrill, Jordan A. Booker, and Robyn Fivush, "Functions of Parental Intergenerational Narratives Told by Young People," *Topics in Cognitive Science* 11, no. 4 (June 21, 2018), https://doi.org/10.1111/tops.12356.

page 45: *The American Academy of Child and Adolescent Psychiatry suggests that under the best of circumstances it can take up to two years for stepfamilies to fully adjust to life together:* "Stepfamily Problems," Facts for Families no. 27, American Academy of Child and Adolescent Psychiatry, updated December 2017, https://www.aacap.org/AACAP/Families_and_Youth/Facts_for_Families/FFF-Guide/Stepfamily-Problems-027.aspx.

page 46: *The American Academy of Pediatrics Committee on Psychosocial Aspects of Child and Family Health advises, "Within stepfamilies, it is unrealistic to hope that the children will immediately respect and love their new stepparents . . .":* "What Your Child is Experiencing When You Remarry," Committee on Psychosocial Aspects of Child and Family Health, American Academy of Pediatrics, updated February 6, 2017, https://www.healthychildren.org/English /family-life/family-dynamics/types-of-families/Pages/What-Your-Child-is -Experiencing-When-You-Remarry.aspx.

page 46: *As the* Landmark *researchers stated, "What most influences the child are the long-term circumstances of life in the postdivorce years.":* Judith Wallerstein, Julia M. Lewis, and Sandra Blakeslee, *The Unexpected Legacy of Divorce: The 25 Year Landmark Study* (New York: Hyperion, 2000).

page 52: The Unexpected Legacy of Divorce: The 25 Year Landmark Study *explains that the father-child relationship has an even greater impact in a divorced family than in a nondivorced one*: Judith Wallerstein, Julia M. Lewis, and Sandra Blakeslee, *The Unexpected Legacy of Divorce: The 25 Year Landmark Study* (New York: Hyperion, 2000).

Page 53: *A 2015 study, published in the* Journal of Marriage and Family, *showed that "Mothers, shouldered the majority of childcare and did not decrease their paid work hours. . . .":* Jill E. Yavorsky, Claire M. Kamp Dush, and Sarah J. Schoppe-Sullivan, "The Production of Inequality: The Gender Division of Labor Across the Transition to Parenthood," *Journal of Marriage and Family* 77, no.3 (April 28, 2015): 662–679, https://doi.org/10.1111/jomf.12189.

page 53: *Even the pandemic lockdown, which forced many dual-career parents to work from home, didn't drastically change the situation*: An April 2020 survey conducted by Morning Consult, a business intelligence agency cited in Claire Cain Miller, "Nearly Half of Men Say They Do Most of the Home Schooling. 3 Percent of Women Agree," *New York Times*, May 8, 2020, https://www .nytimes.com/2020/05/06/upshot/pandemic-chores-homeschooling-gender .html.

page 53: *According to the Pew Research Center, in 2011 fathers averaged seven hours per week on childcare*: "Chapter 4: How Mothers and Fathers Spend Their Time," in *Modern Parenthood,* Pew Research Center, March 14, 2013, https://www.pewresearch.org/social-trends/2013/03/14/chapter-4-how-mothers-and-fathers-spend-their-time/.

Chapter 5: Talking to Your Children About Your Divorce and Nesting

page 121: *Stressing the importance of an open dialogue relates to the concept of "potted-plant parenting,"* ... *As a* New York Times *article describes it: "With teenagers, it's not always easy to know how to connect...*": Lisa Damour, "What Do Teenagers Want? Potted Plant Parents," *New York Times*, December 14, 2016, https://www.nytimes.com/2016/12/14/well/family/what-do-teenagers-want-potted-plant-parents.html.

Index

Two-home conventional divorce
background, 1–4, 33–34
effects on adults, 16–20
effects on children, 15–16, 21–28
expectations of fathers, 50–52
expectations of mothers, 53–54
history of, 5–6, 11–16, 25–27
legacy of childhood divorce in
adulthood, 14–16, 25, 28–30
(*See also The Unexpected
Legacy of Divorce: The 25 Year
Landmark Study*)
option to, 5–6, 31 (*See also*
Nesting)
parenting responsibilities and, 20,
23–25, 50–54

Unanticipated hurdles, 249–251
*The Unexpected Legacy of Divorce:
The 25 Year Landmark
Study* (Wallerstein, Lewis
& Blakeslee), 15–16, 21–23,
24–25, 41–42, 46, 52

Wallerstein, Judith: *The Unexpected
Legacy of Divorce* (*Landmark
Study* with Lewis & Blakeslee),
15–16, 21–23, 24–25, 41–42,
46, 52
Ways to nest, 36–37, 61–79, 86–87.
See also Living arrangements
for nesting
Well-being
emotional, 198–203, 248–249
physical, 198–199, 204–205,
249–251
Wright, Réa
on agreeing to nest, 88
on asking for practical help,
175
on communication, 95
on dating and introducing new
partners, 251, 254, 255
on talking to the children, 91,
113, 118, 119–120, 123
on telling friends and family, 168,
171, 175

About the Author

Beth Behrendt is a mother of three, a freelance writer, and the founder of FamilyNesting.Org. Before pursuing a writing career, she was a research librarian in Washington, D.C.

She now lives in her hometown of Fort Wayne, Indiana, where she and her ex-husband have been nesting with their three children since 2014. Their oldest is now in college, the middle in high school, and the youngest in middle school. She has shared the story of her family's nesting co-parenting in *The New York Times*, *Psychology Today*, and other publications and websites. She regularly writes for *Divorce Magazine* on the topic of nesting and has been a guest on the *Good Divorce*; *Divorcing Well*; *Divorce & Beyond*; and *Thank You, Heartbreak* podcasts. Beth and her ex-husband, Bill, appeared on *Good Morning America* in June 2019 as part of its series on marriage and divorce.

You can subscribe to her mailing list at FamilyNesting.Org and follow her on Facebook, Instagram, Twitter, TikTok, and Pinterest.